SOPHOCLES · II

Ajax
The Women of Trachis
Electra
Philoctetes

THE COMPLETE GREEK TRAGEDIES

Edited by David Grene and Richmond Lattimore

SOPHOCLES · II

AJAX
Translated by John Moore

THE WOMEN OF TRACHIS
Translated by Michael Jameson

ELECTRA
Translated by David Grene

PHILOCTETES
Translated by David Grene

THE UNIVERSITY OF CHICAGO PRESS

CHICAGO & LONDON

The University of Chicago Press, Chicago 60637
The University of Chicago Press, Ltd., London

LCN: 54-10731
ISBN: 0-226-30786-7

♾ The paper used in this publication meets the minimum
requirements of the American National Standard for
Information Sciences—Permanence of Paper for Printed
Library Materials, ANSI Z39.48-1992.

TABLE OF CONTENTS

Ajax / 1

The Women of Trachis / 63

Electra / 121

Philoctetes / 189

AJAX

Translated by John Moore

INTRODUCTION TO *AJAX*

The *Ajax* is probably the earliest of the seven plays by Sophocles which are preserved. The *Antigone* is generally thought to have been produced in 442 or 441 B.C., and the *Ajax* appears to belong to the same period of Sophocles' work. In dramatic technique these plays have not the suppleness of the *Oedipus*, but they are in no sense to be regarded as immature works. At the time he produced the *Antigone*, Sophocles was already fifty-five years old and had been producing tragedies in the Theatre of Dionysus for a quarter of a century. The *Ajax*, too, is the work not of a novice but of a seasoned dramatist. It is a play of very remarkable beauties and likewise of some perplexities.

The subject which Sophocles has chosen is the shame and death of Ajax, which follow on his defeat in the contest for Achilles' armor, and the growth, in and after this shame and death and triumphing over them, of a revealed sense of his heroic virtue and magnanimity. It will be seen that this subject is a single subject: the death of Ajax, taken quite simply in itself, completes nothing; the play's action is complete only when the spectator is brought to an altered estimate of the meaning of Ajax' career and destiny.

Throughout the drama, Ajax remains the central issue and our principal concern. Sophocles' judgment of him is not simple: he sees that Ajax and the Ajax-world of value and aspiration have their limitations in point of sympathy and insight; and the sense of these limitations is in part conveyed to us by means of the figure of Odysseus. Yet to imagine, as some writers have done, that the structure of the play is a polarity, so to speak, between Ajax and Odysseus is surely a distortion. The major dramatic subject, the weight and heft of it, is Ajax. The greatness of his demand upon life is the thing that we must, above all, be made to feel; and Sophocles places this theme before us by the full dramatization he gives of Ajax' suffering and resolution, of the dismay and pathetic dependence of those around him, and of their desolation when his protection is removed.

Sophocles' version of the myth is not original with him; he chose it from among the epic treatments which were already familiar. It is interesting, though, that he chose the version of the story which is most discreditable to Ajax. Pindar, writing a generation before Sophocles, follows a different version in which there is no hint of any attempt by Ajax to murder the Greek chieftains, no lunacy, and no assault upon the livestock. Ajax is simply filled with chagrin because of his disappointment and falls upon his sword. This version suited Pindar's artistic purpose very well: it provided him with a single arresting picture of outraged merit which could serve for a telling allusion and no more. For a dramatist, though, there were richer possibilities in the ghastlier version of the story which emphasized Ajax' criminality and disgrace. In choosing this version Sophocles incurred one serious embarrassment: his hero has *ex hypothesi* been guilty of a foul and treacherous attempt to assassinate the men who have wronged him, and in the prosecution of his plan he has come to grief in a most unseemly way. Sophocles surmounts the difficulty with his usual dexterity. He contrives in the main to make us lose sight of Ajax' criminality, while making of his ignominy a capital dramatic resource. The disclosure of Ajax in his tent, fouled by the animals he has insanely tormented and killed, is more than a powerful *coup de théâtre;* it is a fearful and summary image of total degradation not merely of heroic, but of all human, value. The process by which this image is transformed and Ajax' disaster irradiated by his recovery of heroic strength and human relatedness is the true action of the play.

This process is already well begun by the end of the long scene in which Ajax is disclosed among the slaughtered animals. The scene ends harshly, and, indeed, it is marked throughout by a certain acerbity. Nevertheless, out of his chagrin and misery Ajax is able to reaffirm some part of his former image of himself: rather than endure disgrace, he is resolved to die. There is a moment of tenderness for Eurysaces, none at all for Tecmessa; and even the address to Eurysaces, one feels, is an uncompromising assertion of the quality of Ajax more than a response to the child.

In the next scene he appears an altered man. Not wholly so: his purpose is unchanged. But he discovers in himself, rather to his surprise, a softening of his former harshness. He is touched now by the plight of his wife and child; they must be deceived, so that he may have an opportunity of doing in peace what he has to do; but he deceives them tenderly, expressing his true intentions, but in ambiguous words which they are bound to misunderstand. Thus the speech is a farewell to them, while at the same time it expresses a new attitude in him. His suicide is not to be a frantic gesture of despair: it will be performed composedly, on the seashore, and, when the act is done, he, or something of him, will be saved (sesômenon). The softening of temper which this scene registers is therefore a necessary step in the development of the drama; and the splendid lines in which Ajax compares the softening of his own severity to the yielding of the great stern things in Nature before their gentler opposites have a deep psychological appropriateness.

The scenes which now follow are an impressive example of Sophocles' skill in dramatic organization. As Ajax leaves, sword in hand, bent as we know upon suicide, the Chorus break into an ecstatic song of joy, for they have been deceived by Ajax' words no less than Tecmessa and Eurysaces. At once the messenger arrives with news of the alarming prognostications of Calchas: if Ajax has left his tent, there is no hope for him. Joy and relief are now replaced by terror; Tecmessa understands that she has been deceived; and she and the Chorus in great agitation leave the scene, in haste to forestall Ajax' death.

But Ajax appears, calmly making his preparations (we understand that the scene has changed, as it does sometimes, though rarely, in Greek tragedy—we are now in the place Ajax has chosen by the shore). His death speech is long, eloquent, and handsome. He prays for a quiet death and for his body to be discovered first by Teucer; he calls the Sun-God to carry the news to his home, and the Erinyes to pursue his enemies; and, lastly, he makes his farewell to the world above and his addresses to the world below. Athena is not present by even a mention to disturb the harmonious order of the scene. True, he does not forgive his enemies: to forgive your enemies when you are dying and they surviving is an impulse which lies outside the ethical universe of Sophocles, unless there is a hint of it, and that doubtful, in *Antigone*.

Upon this splendid and now silent solitude Tecmessa and the Chorus urgently break in: the search, the discovery, the broken-hearted cries of grief come rapidly, one upon the other. Those whom Ajax has left are now helpless. They are threatened in every conceivable way; they cannot vindicate Ajax or protect themselves. Only for us Tecmessa's beautiful words (which this translator is helpless to render) may express a portion of the response that seems to be appropriate. Evidently the drama cannot end here; and if Sophocles has not found an entirely happy solution to the problem of how to conclude it, that is not because no conclusion was necessary. Beyond question, we attend to the long wrangle between Teucer and the Atridae with a sense of diminished tragic feeling, not, however, for the reason that the question of Ajax' burial cannot concern us but because the mode selected or enforced upon Sophocles here, that of the set debate, entails a disastrous lowering of tone. The right argument for burial is Odysseus' argument, not Teucer's; and in the *Antigone* the heroine makes no corresponding defense of Polynices.

The *Ajax* has, then, its imperfections and defects. The role of Athena is perplexing, not to say fiendish. Sophocles ignores with perhaps somewhat too ready a skill our repugnance at Ajax' conduct. The wrangle at the end seems unduly prolonged and at times undignified. But all this counts for little in comparison with the admirable and central virtue of the *Ajax*, its sustained and noble affirmation of the heroic in human life, as expressed in Ajax himself, and its rendering in Tecmessa of the beauty of entire devotion.

In making this translation I have followed the text of Sir Richard Jebb.

CHARACTERS

Athena

Odysseus

Ajax

Chorus of Salaminian Sailors

Tecmessa

Messenger

Teucer

Menelaus

Agamemnon

AJAX

SCENE: *Before the "tent" of Ajax, a fairly considerable structure covered
with canvas and equipped with a large principal door and a second
door on the flank, which gives access to a lower lateral extension of
the structure. As the play opens, the goddess Athena is revealed on
a high platform which may be conveniently placed over the lateral
extension of the tent. Odysseus enters and moves eagerly across the
stage as though tracing footprints.*

Athena

    Odysseus, I have always seen and marked you
    Stalking to pounce upon your enemies;
    And now by the tent of Ajax, where he keeps
    Last place upon the shore, I find you busy
    Tracing and scanning these fresh tracks of his,
    New-printed on the sand, to guess if he's inside.
    . You've coursed him like a keen Laconian hound.
    In fact, he has just come in. His head is moist with sweat,
    His murderous hands are moistened too. . . . But now   10
    You need not go on peering in—no, tell me,
    What is the reason for your eager search?
    For I have knowledge and can set you right.

Odysseus

    Voice of Athena, dearest utterance
    Of all the gods' to me—I cannot see you,
    And yet how clearly I can catch your words,
    That speak as from a trumpet's throat of bronze!
    You guess my purpose; I have been circling
    Steadily on the trail of a man I hate,
    Shield-bearing Ajax.   20
    He has done a thing—sometime last night it was—
    An act of staggering horror . . . aimed at us,

If it all can be believed; nothing about it
Is surely known—we are floundering in conjecture,
And I have volunteered to search it out.
This much is sure: we found not long ago
Our flocks and herds of captured beasts all ruined
And struck with havoc by some butchering hand.
Their guards were slaughtered with them. Everyone
Puts the blame of it on Ajax. One man saw him
Alone, bounding over the plain and carrying 30
A sword still wet with blood—this man informed me
And set me on the track. I leapt to the scent
At once; and partly I can trace it still,
Though partly, too, I'm baffled. How can these prints be his?
You come just as I need you. Now and always,
As heretofore, your hand shall be my guide.

Athena

I know, Odysseus;
Some time ago I felt your need and came
On the path to guard and help you in your chase.

Odysseus

Tell me, dear mistress: am I working to some purpose?

Athena

Yes, this is the man that did the things you speak of.

Odysseus

What motive, though, prompted that senseless hand? 40

Athena

He was aggrieved, because of Achilles' armor.

Odysseus

But why this wild assault upon the flocks?

Athena

Ah, he thought it was your murder that fouled his hands.

Odysseus

It was a stroke, then, aimed at the whole Greek army?

Athena
A successful one, if I had not been watchful.

Odysseus
What desperate daring nerved him to the thing?

Athena
In the night he was moving upon you, stealthily and alone.

Odysseus
Did he come close? Was he reaching near his goal?

Athena
To the very doors of the two supreme commanders.

Odysseus
And how did he check that hand that yearned for murder?   50

Athena
I checked him; I threw before his eyes
Obsessive notions, thoughts of insane joy,
To fall on the mingled droves of captured livestock,
The undistributed loot which the herdsmen had in charge.
He hit them,
Hewed out a weltering shambles of horned beasts,
Cleaving them down in a circle all around him.
Sometimes he thought he held the sons of Atreus
In his grip to kill them, and then again
His fancy would seize some other of the chiefs.
The man was wandering in diseased delusions;
I pressed him, urged him into the fatal net.
At last, when he was weary of the slaughter,   60
He hobbled the cattle that were still alive,
And the sheep, and brought them to his tent, thinking
It was men he had captured and not poor horned beasts.
And now he has them bound inside the lodge
And is tormenting them. But I shall show you
His madness in plain view. Take note of it;
Then you can publish it to all the Greeks.

(Odysseus shrinks back.)

Get a grip on your nerves and wait. It's no disaster
To see the man. I'll turn his glance away.   70
He'll never see you or know your face. Halloo!
You there, who are binding fast your captives' arms
With fetters, come outside! Ajax! Come out!

Odysseus

Athena, what can you be thinking of?
Don't call him out!

Athena

Quiet, now! No cowardice!

Odysseus

No, no, for heaven's sake!
I'd very much rather he stayed inside.

Athena

What are you afraid of? He was only a man before.

Odysseus

Yes, but he was my enemy and still is.

Athena

But to laugh at your enemies—
What sweeter laughter can there be than that?

Odysseus

It's enough for me if he stays just where he is.   80

Athena

You're afraid, then, to see a madman face to face?

Odysseus

Certainly if he were sane, I should never shrink from him.

Athena

No need to do so now. He will stand near you,
And yet not see you.

Odysseus

How is that possible, if he sees with the same eyes still?

Athena

I can darken even the most brilliant vision.

Odysseus

I know that a god's contriving may do anything.

Athena

Be still, then, and remain right where you are.

Odysseus

If I must, I must. But I wish I were anywhere but here!

Athena

Ajax, I call you once again!

Is this how much you care for your old ally?   90

> (*Ajax enters through the principal door of the tent, carrying a*
> *two-thonged leather whip.*)

Ajax

Hail, Athena! Daughter of Zeus,

Hail and welcome! How well you have stood by me!

I shall deck you with trophies all of gold

From the spoils of this hunting, in thanksgiving.

Athena

Excellent. But tell me, did you dip

Your blade well in the Greeks' blood?

Ajax

I think I may boast as much. I don't deny it.

Athena

Did you move your weaponed hand against the generals?

Ajax

I don't think they will slight Ajax again.

Athena

The men are dead, if I understand you correctly.

Ajax

Dead they are. Let them rob my armor now!   100

Athena

Tell me, please, what happened to Laertes' son?
He didn't escape you?

Ajax

Oho, that villainous sneak! You want to know where *he* is?

Athena

Yes. Your adversary, you know. Odysseus.

Ajax

He's sitting there inside, my sweetest prisoner.
I don't intend for him to die just yet.

Athena

What are you going to do first?

Ajax

First bind him to the pole that props my barrack.

Athena

Poor miserable man! What treatment will you give him?

Ajax

Crimson his back with this whip first, then kill him.   110

Athena

Poor wretch! In pity don't mistreat him so!

Ajax

Have your way, goddess, in all else, and welcome.
But that man's punishment shall not be changed.

Athena

Well, then, if your good pleasure wills it so,
Do execution, carry out all you have in mind.

Ajax

I must be at my work. Goddess, I grant you this:
Stand always my ally as you have today.

(*Exit.*)

Athena

Do you see, Odysseus, how great the gods' power is?

Who was more full of foresight than this man,
Or abler, do you think, to act with judgment? 120

Odysseus

None that I know of. Yet I pity
His wretchedness, though he is my enemy,
For the terrible yoke of blindness that is on him.
I think of him, yet also of myself;
For I see the true state of all us that live—
We are dim shapes, no more, and weightless shadow.

Athena

Look well at this, and speak no towering word
Yourself against the gods, nor walk too grandly
Because your hand is weightier than another's,
Or your great wealth deeper founded. One short day 130
Inclines the balance of all human things
To sink or rise again. Know that the gods
Love men of steady sense and hate the proud.

(Exeunt.)
(Enter the Chorus of Salaminian sailors.)

Chorus

Son of Telamon, lord of the firm floor
Of Salamis, where the sea chafes and swirls,
Ajax, my lord,
When you are fortunate, I too feel gladness;
But when the fury of Zeus or the virulent
Slur of the Greeks' slander
Strikes you, I shrink in fear, and my eye
Like a bird's, like a dove's, shows terror. 140
Now out of this fading night
Come huge oppressive rumors of dismay,
Wretched and shameful;
For you, they say, in the dark went striding out
Over the horse-delighting grassland,
Swinging your bright sword, slaughtering and wasting
All that remained of booty,

Flocks and herds belonging to the host.
Such tales as these, whisperings and fabrications,
Odysseus is supplying to every ear,
And many believe him. For as he speaks of you,   150
His words win credit, and each new hearer
More than the teller relishes his chance
To insult at your distress.
Strike at a great man, and you will not miss;
But if one should bend such slander at me,
None would believe him. Envy stalks
After magnates of wealth and power;
Yet humble men without their princes
Are a frail prop for a fortress. They
Should be dependent upon the great,   160
And the great be upheld by lesser ones.
But the shallow cannot be taught these things—
They raise instead an ignorant clamor;
And against it we have no defense, my lord,
But you. When once they are out of your sight,
They screech like a gaggle of angry birds;
But fear of the huge falcon,
All of a sudden, I think,
If you should only appear,   170
Would make them cower and be still.

Strophe

Can it have been wild, bull-consorting Artemis
   That stirred you, evil Tale,
Mother of my disgrace, to move against the flocks?
   Was she angered perhaps for victory-dues unpaid,
   Or disappointed of rich captured arms,
   Or hunting recompense for a stag slain?
Or was it Enyalios, the bronze-cased Lord of War
   That blamed *our* lord's co-operant spear,
And spitefully paid him out in the night's error?   180

Antistrophe

For never, son of Telamon, of your own heart's prompting,
   Would you so far have strayed
To fall upon the flocks. Yet Frenzy comes
When the gods will. Apollo and Zeus forfend
   These tales be true that the Greeks are spreading!
     Yet if the high kings
   Or Sisyphus' execrated son
Weave with false art a supposititious tale,   190
     Guard us from that false speech—
Hide not, so, your face in your tent beside the sea.

Epode

Rise, up from the place
Where you sit so obdurate, forbearing to fight your cause,
   While ruin flares toward heaven,
   And your enemies' bold outrage
   Freshens through all the glades
In a blast of ringing laughter and hard spite.
   But I am fixed in my grief.   200

(Enter Tecmessa from the tent.)

Tecmessa

Mariners who serve with Ajax,
Our prince of the old and kingly line
Sprung from Athenian earth, we
Who care for him and his father's far-off home
Have cause indeed for grief;
For he, our great grim man of power, lies low,
And a troubling flood is on him.

Chorus

But what, succeeding to yesterday's
Load of wretchedness, has this night brought?
Tell us, daughter of Phrygian Teleutas;   210
For the valiant Ajax loves you,
And honors his spear-won bride—
Being near him, perhaps you have knowledge and can speak.

Tecmessa

But how shall I speak a thing that appalls my speech?
You shall hear too clearly of an accident
Awful as death.
Madness has seized our noble Ajax;
He has come to ignominy in the night.
What a sight is to be seen within the tent!
Victims, slain with his own hand, deep in blood,
As for an oracle, speakingly reveal him.   220

Chorus

   Strophe

You have vouched it true, then, that report of our fiery chief,
That tale we cannot bear, yet may not escape:
Huge it grows, and authoritative voices
Give it huge reinforcement. Oh, I fear
For that which is moving upon us. He will be done to death,
Our glorious prince, because
With frenzied hands and a dark sword he slew   230
Herds and their mounted guardians in a heap.

Tecmessa

Alas, then, it can only have been from there
That he brought those bound beasts home!
And some he slew on the tent's floor
Cleanly with a neck-cut; others he hacked asunder
With slashes at their ribs. But two special
White-footed rams he lifted up, shore off
One's head and the tip of its tongue, and cast them from him;
The other he bound upright against a pillar,   240
Seized a stout length of harness, made from it
A singing whip, two-thonged, to lash him with,
And, mid the blows, poured forth such awful curses
As no man, but some demon, must have taught him.

Chorus

   Antistrophe

Now is the time for a man to muffle his head

And over the land to urge his stealthy way,
Or else, sitting the thwarts to row,
To trust his life to a ship's swift course on the deep—   250
Such are the threats that the sons of Atreus, two in power,
Stir toward us. I am in dread to share
With him the blows and hurt of the killing stone;
For an awful thing to be near is the doom that holds him.

Tecmessa

No longer so. After the lightning
Flash and leap of the storm-wind,
He is calm. But now, being clear in mind,
He is freshly miserable. It is a painful thing
To look at your own trouble and know   260
That you yourself and no one else has made it.

Chorus

But still, if his fit is past, I should think he was lucky;
A seizure, once it is done with, matters less.

Tecmessa

If someone posed the question, which would you choose:
To grieve your friends while feeling joy yourself,
Or to be wretched with them, shares alike?

Chorus

The last, lady, is twice as bad a thing.

Tecmessa

We are ill no longer now, but merely ruined.

Chorus

What do you mean? I cannot understand you.   270

Tecmessa

Ajax, so long as the mad fit was on him,
Himself felt joy at all his wretchedness,
Though we, his sane companions, grieved indeed.
But now that he's recovered and breathes clear,
His own anguish totally masters him,

While we are no less wretched than before.
Is not this a redoubling of our grief?

Chorus

You are quite right. Lady, I wonder
If a fearful blow of God's anger may have hit him.
It is strange that he feels no happier sane than raving.   280

Tecmessa

Strange, perhaps. But the facts are as they are.

Chorus

How at the start did this catastrophe
Swoop down? Tell us: we share the pain of it.

Tecmessa

Indeed, you are partners and shall hear it all.
In the depth of night, after the evening flares
Had all gone out, Ajax, with sword in hand,
Went slowly groping toward the door, intent
Upon some pointless errand. I objected,
And said, "Ajax, what are you doing? Why
Do you stir? No messenger has summoned you: 290
You have heard no trumpet. Why, the whole army now's
    asleep!"
He answered briefly in a well-worn phrase,
"Woman, a woman's decency is silence."
I heard, and said no more; he issued forth alone.
I don't know what horrors occurred outside,
But when he came back in, he brought with him
A mass of hobbled bulls and shepherd dogs
And woolly captives. He struck the heads off some;
Others' he severed with an upward cut;
And some, held fast in bonds, he kept abusing
With words and blows, as though they were human beings—
And all the while he was vexing poor dumb beasts.   300
At length he darted out the door and spoke
Wild, rending words, directed toward some phantom,
Exulting with a harsh laugh *how he'd paid them,*
Odysseus and the sons of Atreus. Then

He sprang back in again, and somehow, slowly,
By painful stages came to his right mind.
And when he saw his dwelling full of Ruin,
He beat his head and bellowed. There he sat,
Wreckage himself among the wreck of corpses,
The sheep slaughtered; and in an anguished gripe
Of fist and fingernail he clutched his hair.   310
He sat so, without speaking, for some time;
Then finally spoke those fearful, threatening words—
What should befall me if I failed to say
What had befallen him: he asked me where he stood.
Friends, I was terrified by all he'd done,
And told him, simply, everything I knew.
Then he cried out—long wails of shattering pain,
Like none I ever heard from him before;
He always used to say such cries were base,
Marks of an abject spirit. His own way   320
Was not to cry aloud in his distress,
But low and muffled, like a roaring bull.
Now, though, quite overcome by his misfortune,
Refusing food and drink, he sits there motionless,
Relapsed among the beasts his iron brought down.
There are clear signs, too,
That he's aiming to do some dreadful thing; his words
And his lamentations both somehow suggest it.
Friends—this was the thing I came to ask of you—
Won't you come in and comfort him, if you can?
He is noble, and may listen to his friends.   330

Chorus

Honored Tecmessa, what a fearful frenzy,
By your account, his griefs have moved him to!

> (*Ajax inside the tent gives a heavy groan, which rises
> slowly almost to a shriek.*)

Tecmessa

Worse may be coming. Didn't you hear his voice,
Ajax', distorted in that ghastly cry?

(Ajax groans again miserably.)

Chorus

Either he still is mad, or else can't bear
The company his madness made around him

Ajax (within)

Boy! Where is my child?

Tecmessa

Dear God! Eurysaces, it's you he's calling.   340
What can he want? Where are you? What shall I do?

Ajax (within)

Teucer! Where are you? Where is my brother Teucer?
Will that raid of his last forever? And I here perishing!

Chorus

No, he seems to be sane. Open the door.
Perhaps seeing someone, though it's only us,
May help him to compose himself.

*Tecmessa (opens the door, revealing Ajax sitting dejectedly in the
    middle of slaughtered bulls and sheep)*

There, now you see.
You can judge for yourself the state of his affairs,
And how the man is too.

Ajax

Ah!
Loved mariners, my only friends,
Still faithful in the old proved way,   350
Look at this swirling tide of grief
    And the storm of blood behind it,
      Coursing around and round me.

Chorus

Horrible!
Tecmessa, what you told us was too true—
Insanity stands here revealed indeed!

Ajax

    Antistrophe

  Ah!

  Stout hearts and skilful seamen,

  Strong hands to move the oar,

  I see no friend but you,

  No, none, to ease my pain.   360

  For God's sake, help me die!

Chorus

  Hush! Check those awful words!

  Don't seek a worse cure for an ill disease,

  And make your pain still heavier than it is.

Ajax

    Strophe

  Here I am, the bold, the valiant,

  Unflinching in the shock of war,

  A terrible threat to unsuspecting beasts.

  Oh! what a mockery I have come to! What indignity!

Tecmessa

  Ajax, my lord and master,

  I beg you not to say such things.

Ajax

  Go away! Take yourself out of my sight!   370

                                (He groans.)

Chorus

  In God's name, be more gentle and more temperate.

Ajax

  How could I be so cursed?

  To let those precious villains out of my hand,

  And fall on goats and cattle,

  On crumpled horns and splendid flocks,

  Shedding their dark blood!

Chorus

  The thing is done. Why wail about it now?

  You cannot make it undone.

Ajax

   Antistrophe

Ah, yes, son of Laertes

Spying everywhere, always   380

The tool of every mischief,

Filthiest scoundrel of all the army,

What a huge laugh you're laughing now, what gloating!

Chorus

It is God's giving if we laugh or weep.

Ajax

Ah, if I could just once catch sight of him!

Crushed as I am, I'd . . .

Chorus (interrupting)

My lord, no blustering words.

Your situation's desperate; can't you see?

Ajax

Zeus, father of my fathers,

How can I strike them down,

That devious, hateful rogue and the two joined kings,   390

And last find death myself?

Tecmessa

When you pray that prayer, why, pray for my death too;

Why should I live when once my lord is dead?

Ajax

   Strophe

O

Darkness that is my light,

Murk of the underworld, my only brightness,

Oh, take me to yourself to be your dweller,

Receive and keep me. I cannot look

To any of the race of gods for help,

Being no longer worthy,

Nor yet to humankind.   400

But the martial goddess, daughter of Zeus, cruelly works my ruin.

Where shall a man flee?
Where shall I turn for refuge?
All that I was has perished
With these poor creatures here,
And I abused by a fool's dream
Of stalk and capture. Friends, friends,
The massed army will take my life
With bloody insistent blows.

Tecmessa

What wretchedness, to hear a brave man speak   410
Such words as once he would not deign to use!

Ajax

   Antistrophe

O
Sounding straits of the sea
Caves by the sea's edge, meadows on the shore,
Long and long have you kept me here in Troyland;
But now I shall not revive again, never again—
A man of sense may know it.
Scamander, neighboring river, gentle to Greeks,   420
You shall no longer see this man,
Such a man (let me now speak my boast)
As Troy ne'er saw the like of, not in all
The warlike host that hither came from Greece.
But now in dishonor
I lie abject.

Chorus

I cannot bid you stifle such great griefs;
And yet it is agony to hear your grieving.

Ajax

Agony. Who would have thought my name and fortune   430
Could square so well together! My name is Ajax:
Agony is its meaning. And my fortunes
Are cause indeed for an agony of wailing,

Cause and enough twice over. How my father,
Fighting here under Ida long ago,
Won with his sword the loveliest prize of all
For valor, and sweet praise at his return;
But I, his son,
Coming in my turn with a force no less
To this same land of Troy, no less than he a champion,
Nor less deserving, yet am left an outcast,
Shamed by the Greeks, to perish as I do!   440
And yet I seem to know this simple truth:
If the bestowing of the famous armor
Had rested with Achilles while he lived,
To give them as a war-prize to the bravest,
No rival then would have filched them from my hands;
But now the sons of Atreus have contrived
That a man of most dishonest mind should have them,
Pushing my claims aside. And I say this,
That if my eyes and mind had not leapt whirling
Wide from my aim, those two would never again
Cheat anyone with their awards and ballots!
But, instead, the fierce-eyed, overpowering   450
Daughter of Zeus, just then as I was readying
My hand and plot against them, set me sprawling,
Distraught and frenzied, and I dipped my hands
In the blood of beasts like these. And now they are laughing
And triumph in their clear escape, which I
Never intended for them. But when God
Strikes harm, a worse man often foils his better.
And now, Ajax—what is to be done now?
I am hated by the gods, that's plain; the Greek camp hates me:
Troy and the ground I stand upon detest me.
Shall I go, then, from this place where the ships ride,   460
Desert the Atridae, and cross the Aegean to my home?
But when I'm there,
What countenance can I show my father Telamon?
How will he ever stand the sight of me

If I come before him naked, armed with no glory,
When he himself won chaplets of men's praise?
That won't bear thinking of. Well, then,
Shall I make a rush against the walls of Troy,
Join with them all in single combat, do
Some notable exploit, and find my death in it?
But that might give some comfort to the sons of Atreus.
No. I must find some better way entirely—   470
An enterprise which will prove to my old father
That the son of his loins is not by breed a weakling.
It's a contemptible thing to want to live forever
When a man's life gives him no relief from trouble.
What joy is there in a long file of days,
Edging you forward toward the goal of death,
Then back again a little? I wouldn't give much for a man
Who warms himself with the comfort of vain hopes.
Let a man nobly live or nobly die
If he *is* a nobleman: I have said what I had to say.   480

Chorus

Ajax, no one could ever call those words
Spurious or alien to you. They are your own heart's speech.
Pause, though, a moment; put aside these thoughts;
And give your friends a chance to win you over.

Tecmessa

Ajax, my master, life knows no harder thing
Than to be at the mercy of compelling fortune.
I, for example, was born of a free father;
If any man in Phrygia was lordly and prosperous, he was.
Now I'm a slave. Such, it seems, was the gods' will,
And the will of your strong hand. But since I've come   490
To share your bed with you, my thoughts are loyal
To you and yours. And I beg you
In the holy name of Zeus who guards your hearth-fire,
And by your bed, in which you have known peace with me,
Don't give me up to hear the harsh speech

Of your enemies and bow to it, their bondslave.
For this is certain: the day you die
And by your death desert me, that same day
Will see me outraged too, forcibly dragged
By the Greeks, together with your boy, to lead a slave's life.
And then some one of the lord class,   500
With a lashing word, will make his hateful comment:
"There she is, Ajax' woman;
He was the greatest man in the whole army.
How enviable her life was then, and now how slavish!"
Some speech in that style. And my ill fate
Will be driving me before it, but these words
Will be a reproach to you and all your race.
Ajax, revere your father; do not leave him
In the misery of his old age—and your mother,
Shareholder in many years, revere her too!
She prays the gods for your safe return, how often!
And last, dear lord, show pity to your child.   510
Robbed of his infant nurture, reft of you,
To live his life out under the rule of guardians
Not kind nor kindred—what a wretchedness
You by your death will deal to him and me!
And I no longer have anywhere to look for help,
If not to you. My country was destroyed
Utterly by your spear, and another fate
Brought down my mother and my father too,
To dwell in death with Hades. Then what fatherland
Shall I ever have but you? Or what prosperity?
You are my only safety. O my lord,
Remember even me. A man ought to remember   520
If he has experienced any gentle thing.
Kindness it is that brings forth kindness always.
But when a man forgets good done to him
And the recollection of it slips away,
How shall I any longer call him noble?

Chorus

    Ajax, I wish you could have pity in your heart
    As I do. For then you might approve her words.

Ajax

    Well, she can certainly count on my approval
    If only she sets her mind to do as I bid her.

Tecmessa

    Dearest Ajax, I will be all obedience.

Ajax

    Then bring me my child and let me see him.   530

Tecmessa

    It was only because of my fears that I removed him.

Ajax

    In all this terrible business? Or do I understand you?

Tecmessa

    For fear the poor little one might come in your way and be killed.

Ajax

    Yes, that would have been worthy of my evil genius.

Tecmessa

    At all events I took care that it shouldn't happen.

Ajax

    You did well and deserve credit for your foresight.

Tecmessa

    Is there anything, then, you want me to do for you?

Ajax

    Yes. Let me speak to my boy and see his face.

Tecmessa

    He's not far off. The servants are looking after him.

Ajax

    Why doesn't he come at once, then?   540

Tecmessa

    Eurysaces! Your father is calling for you.

(To one of the servants inside.)

You bring him! you have him by the hand.

Ajax

Is he coming? Doesn't he hear your words?

(Enter, from the side door, a servant leading
Eurysaces by the hand.)

Tecmessa

Here he is. See, the servant's bringing him.

Ajax

Lift him up, lift him to me. He won't be frightened,
Even by seeing this fresh-butchered gore,
Not if he really is my son. Break in
The colt straight off to his father's rugged ways;
Train him to have a nature like his sire.
My boy, have better luck than your father had,   550
Be like him in all else; and you will not be base.
You know, even now I somewhat envy you:
You have no sense of all this misery.
Not knowing anything's the sweetest life—
Ignorance is an evil free from pain—
Till the time comes when you learn of joy and grief.
And when you come to that,
Then you must show your father's enemies
What sort of a man you are, and what man's son.
Till then feed on light breezes, basking
In the tenderness of your young life, giving your mother joy.
For rest assured, the Greeks will not offer you outrage   560
Or hatefully insult you, even when we are parted.
I leave you a strong warden at the door,
Teucer. He will protect and rear you up
And stint you nothing, even though now he's far away,
Gone on a distant raid in enemy country.
—You, men at arms and seafarers, my followers,
I enjoin this act of kindness on you all:

Pass on my command to Teucer; bid him take
My boy here to my home, present him
To Telamon and my mother, Eriboea,
And let him tend and nourish their old age   570
With constancy, till at the last they find
Their dark apartments with the god below.
As for my arms—
I say no arbiter of the Greeks shall set them
As a prize of competition for the army;
Certainly my destroyer shall not. Rather
You, my boy, take from me this great weapon
From which you have your name, Eurysaces;
Hold and direct it by its stalwart strap,
This sevenfold-oxhide-thick unbreachable shield.
The rest of my armor shall be buried with me.
But there's enough. Come, take the child quickly;
Close up the house. And let there be no wailing
Here out of doors. Lord, what a plaintive creature   580
Womankind is! (*He goes inside.*) Make fast, and hurry!
No good physician quavers incantations
When the malady he's treating needs the knife.

Chorus

I'm terrified by your eager urgency,
And take no comfort in your whetted tongue.

Tecmessa

Ajax, my lord, what is your mind bent upon?

Ajax

Don't probe and question! It becomes you to submit.

Tecmessa

How my heart falters! Ajax, by your child
And by the gods I beg you, don't be our betrayer!

Ajax

You're growing tedious. Don't you know by now
That I owe the gods no service any more?   590

Tecmessa

What impious words!

Ajax

Reprove those who hear you.

Tecmessa

And will you not relent?

Ajax

You've said too much already.

Tecmessa

My lord, it is my fear that speaks!

Ajax (to the servants)

Shut the doors at once!

Tecmessa

In the gods' name, soften!

Ajax

You have a foolish thought
If you think at this late date to school my nature.

> (*The doors are shut; Tecmessa remains quietly crouching
> or kneeling beside them. A servant stands behind her,
> holding Eurysaces by the hand.*)

Chorus

Strophe

O splendid Salamis, my heart recalls,
Blest island, where you lie
At peace in the surf's pounding,
Radiant in all men's sight and prized forever.
But Time has grown old since I   600
Have kept this wretched bivouac under Ida,
Losing count of the months' lapse,
Feeling the slow abrasion;
And dark is my thought's forecast:
Shall I win, shall I yet come, shall my coming be
To the somber and detested house of Death?

Antistrophe

And now wretchedly I must face
A new bout, for Ajax, ill to cure,   610
Sits by, and holy madness is his consort.
You sent him forth, fair island, in a time long past,
A warrior brilliant among warriors. Now
He keeps his thoughts' flock in loneliness
And grieves his friends.
And the works of war that once his strong hands did
Are fallen, fallen,
Undear, unfriended by the friendless kings.   620

Strophe

I think, too,
Of his mother, with the white of age upon her:
Surely when the news of his mind's ravage
Is brought to her (O lamentable! lamentable!)
Not like the poor lorn nightingale
In a low sob will she utter her heart's anguish,
But high, rending strains will break from her,   630
The breast be beaten, and the tresses torn.

Antistrophe

Better if he
Were hidden in Hades, now his mind is gone;
For though his proud lineage
Excelled his warlike peers,
He keeps no more the steady heart we knew,
But ranges in extravagant madness. Wretched father!   640
What a hard word you must hear! Calamity
Fallen upon your son, such as no other
Of all his race has borne, but only he.

(Enter Ajax from the tent with a sword in his hand.)

Ajax

Strangely the long and countless drift of time
Brings all things forth from darkness into light,
Then covers them once more. Nothing so marvelous

That man can say it surely will not be—
Strong oath and iron intent come crashing down.
My mood, which just before was strong and rigid,   650
No dipped sword more so, now has lost its edge—
My speech is womanish for this woman's sake;
And pity touches me for wife and child,
Widowed and lost among my enemies.
But now I'm going to the bathing place
And meadows by the sea, to cleanse my stains,
In hope the goddess' wrath may pass from me.
And when I've found a place that's quite deserted,
I'll dig in the ground, and hide this sword of mine,
Hatefulest of weapons, out of sight. May Darkness
And Hades, God of Death, hold it in their safe keeping.   660
For never, since I took it as a gift
Which Hector, my great enemy, gave to me,
Have I known any kindness from the Greeks.
I think the ancient proverb speaks the truth:
An enemy's gift is ruinous and no gift.
Well, then,
From now on this will be my rule: Give way
To Heaven, and bow before the sons of Atreus.
They are our rulers, they must be obeyed.
I must give way, as all dread strengths give way,
In turn and deference. Winter's hard-packed snow
Cedes to the fruitful summer; stubborn night   670
At last removes, for day's white steeds to shine.
The dread blast of the gale slackens and gives
Peace to the sounding sea; and Sleep, strong jailer,
In time yields up his captive. Shall not I
Learn place and wisdom? Have I not learned this,
Only so much to hate my enemy
As though he might again become my friend,
And so much good to wish to do my friend,   680
As knowing he may yet become my foe?
Most men have found friendship a treacherous harbor.

Enough: this will be well.

You, my wife, go in
And fervently and continually pray the gods
To grant fulfilment of my soul's desire.
And you, my friends, heed my instructions too,
And when he comes, deliver this to Teucer:
Let him take care for me and thought for you.
Now I am going where my way must go;   690
Do as I bid you, and you yet may hear
That I, though wretched now, have found my safety.

> (*Ajax goes out through the wing; Tecmessa
> and Eurysaces go into the tent.*)

Chorus

  Strophe

I shudder and thrill with joy,
I leap and take wings—Lord Pan!
Come to me over the sea
From your huge, snow-buffeted mountain,
From the long, harsh ridge of Cyllênê.
I would dance, I am bent upon dancing!
Teach me (you are the gods' teacher
And yourself you need no teacher)
Wild, high, excited dances, Mysian, Cnosian—   700
I would dance, I am bent upon dancing!
And over the open sea
Come to me in the clear light,
Apollo, Lord of Delos—
Be with me in kindness always.

  Antistrophe

The harsh god has taken
His siege of grief from our eyes.
(I exult with love and with joy!)
Once again, Zeus,
King of the bright air, your perfect daylight
May bathe our skimming seacraft in its whiteness.

Ajax forgets his pain,   710
And now, with holy rite and due observance,
Once more knows reverent thoughts.
Great Time makes all things dim,
And nothing seems beyond the verge of speech,
Since Ajax has resolved
(Amazing!) his heart's fierceness and his stern
Strife with the sons of Atreus.

(Enter a Messenger.)

Messenger

Friends, I would deliver this news first to you:
Teucer has just come back from rugged Mysia.   720
No sooner did he reach headquarters than
The whole Greek army gathered to abuse him.
They'd seen him coming quite a long way off
And, when he arrived, stood around him in a circle,
Jabbing at him with jeers from every side.
Called him the brother of a lunatic
And traitor to the army; threatened him
With stoning to a torn and bloody death.
So far they went that eager fingers then
Had plucked forth swords from scabbards, but the thing,   730
Just as it hurried toward its uttermost,
Grew quiet at the elders' peaceful words.
But where is Ajax? I must speak my charge,
And cannot do it but to my lord himself.

Chorus

He is not here. He went away just now;
His heart is changed, and bends to bear the yoke
Of a changed purpose.

Messenger

         May God help him then!
Perhaps the man that sent me was too slow
In sending, or I lingered on the way.

Chorus

What is so urgent? Why do you think you're late?   740

Messenger

    Teucer declared the man should not go out,
    But stay indoors, till he himself arrives.

Chorus

    He *has* gone out, though—seeking his truest good.
    He wants to be relieved of the gods' anger.

Messenger

    A very foolish and misguided thought,
    If Calchas can foresee events at all!

Chorus

    What are you saying? What can you know of it?

Messenger

    This much I know—I happened to be near:
    For Calchas rose and left the kingly circle   750
    And came to speak with Teucer privately
    Without the Atridae; gently he placed his hand
    In Teucer's own, and urged and pled with him
    To use all shifts to keep his brother safe
    Under his tent-roof, and confine him there
    Throughout the length of this now present day,
    If ever he wished to see him alive again.
    Only for this one day, the prophet said,
    Will the Goddess Athena vex him with her anger.
    "Wherever men forget their mere man's nature,
    Thinking a thought too high, they have no use
    Of their huge bulk and boldness, but they fall   760
    On most untoward disasters sent by Heaven.
    Ajax, even when he first set out from home,
    Proved himself foolish, when his father gave him
    His good advice at parting. 'Child,' he said,
   'Resolve to win, but always with God's help.'
    But Ajax answered with a senseless boast:
   'Father, with God's help even a worthless man
    Could triumph. I propose, without that help,
    To win my prize of fame.' In such a spirit

He boasted. And when once Athena stood   770
Beside him in the fight, urging him on
To strike the enemy with his deadly hand,
He answered then, that second time, with words
To shudder at, not speak: 'Goddess,' he said,
'Go stand beside the other Greeks; help them.
For where I bide, no enemy will break through.'
These were the graceless words which won for him
The goddess' wrath; they kept no human measure.
But if he lives this day out, then perhaps,
With God's help, we may be his saviors still."
This was the seer's message. Teucer rose   780
At once and sent me off, bearing you these
Instructions, with strict charge to keep them. But
If Ajax has deprived me of my hope,
His life is done. Else Calchas has no art.

Chorus

Tecmessa, I think you were born for every misery.
Come and attend to this man's fearful story.

(As though to himself.)

The razor grazes near, and I feel no comfort.

(Enter Tecmessa, carrying Eurysaces.)

Tecmessa

I have only just found respite from that other
Siege of calamities. What new alarm is this?

Chorus

Listen to the message this man has brought.
It concerns Ajax, and it sounds grim.   790

Tecmessa

Alas, what *is* your message? Not that we're ruined?

Messenger

As to your own case, I can't say. But if Ajax
Has left his tent, there is not much hope for him.

Tecmessa

But he *has* gone out. I tremble in suspense
To know your meaning.

Messenger

Teucer sends strict directions that Ajax
Must be kept under the cover of his tent
And not permitted to go out alone.

Tecmessa

But where *is* Teucer? And why does he say this?

Messenger

He has just returned. And he apprehends
That Ajax' going out will be his ruin.

Tecmessa

Heaven help us! Who was the man that told him this?   800

Messenger

Calchas the prophet. He warned us to be on our guard
All day, for it brings him either life or death.

Tecmessa

Alas, friends, stand between me and my doom!
Hurry, some of you, and bring Teucer quickly;
The rest divide—let one group search the eastward
And one the westward bendings of the shore,
To trace his dangerous path. I can see now
That I have been beguiled of his intent
And exiled from his kindness which I knew.
But oh! my child, what shall I do? Not stay,
But join the search as far as my strength supports me.   810
Come, let's be at the work! No time to linger,
If we aim to save a man that's bent on death.

Chorus

I am ready. More than my words shall show it.
You'll find me swift of foot and prompt in action.

*(Tecmessa leaves Eurysaces with the attendants and goes
hurriedly out. Meanwhile, the Chorus divides into
two equal semichoruses and exits through the
side entrances.)*

SCENE: *An empty place by the seashore. No scenery need be indicated
except some bushes, behind which Ajax' body will fall. His preparations, though, should be largely visible to the audience. Enter
Ajax.*

*Ajax (carefully fixes the sword in place, tamps down the ground, and feels
the edge of the blade)*

He's firm in the ground, my Slayer. And his cut
(If I have time even for this reflection)
Should now be deadliest. For, first, the sword
Was Hector's gift, a token of guest-friendship,
And he of all guest-friends my bitterest foe;
Here, too, it stands, lodged in this hostile ground
Of Troy, its edge made new with iron-devouring stone.   820
And, last, I've propped it, so, with careful handling,
To help me soon and kindly to my death.
This preparation I have made. And now,
Making my invocation, as is right,
I call first, Zeus, on you. Grant me a little thing:
Rouse up some messenger for me, to bear
The news of my disaster first to Teucer,
So that he first may gently lift me up
When I have fallen on this reeking sword.
I would not have some enemy spy me out
And cast me forth, a prize for birds and dogs.   830
Grant me, O Zeus, this one thing. And do you,
Hermes, Conductor to the Nether World,
Waft me with one swift unconvulsive leap
Upon this piercing blade. And you, Dread Furies—
You who are ever maidens and do watch
Above all fates and sufferings of men—

Come with long strides, my helpers; mark my end,
How Atreus' sons have brought me to my ruin,
And sweep upon them for their ruin too.
They see me falling now by my own hand; 840
So too by loved and kindred hand may they!
Go, swift and punishing Erinyes,
Taste the whole army's blood, and spare them nothing.
And you that drive your chariot up the steep
Of Heaven, Lord Helios—when you next shall see
My own dear country, check your golden reins,
And bring the tale of my distressful death
To my old father and to her that nursed me.
Poor mother! When she hears this wretched word, 850
How her grief's note will quaver through the town!
But I must leave this idle vein of weeping
And set about my business with some speed.
Strong God of Death, attend me now and come.
And yet I shall converse with you hereafter
And know you in the world below. But you,
Sweet gleam of daylight now before my eyes,
And Sun-God, splendid charioteer, I greet you
For this last time and never any more.
O radiance, O my home and hallowed ground
Of Salamis, and my father's hearth, farewell! 860
And glorious Athens, and my peers and kin
Nurtured with me, and here all springs and streams,
My nurses, you that wet the plains of Troy,
Farewell! This last word Ajax gives to you;
The rest he keeps, to speak among the dead.

(He falls on the sword and collapses behind the bushes.
Enter, from one wing, the first of the two divisions
of the Chorus.)

First Semichorus
   Toil breeds toil upon toil,
   Where, where have I not searched?

No place knows that I share its secret.
Listen! What noise was that?   870

(Enter, from the other wing, the other division
of the Chorus.)

Second Semichorus
Only us, your shipmates.

First Semichorus
What luck?

Second Semichorus
From the ships to westward we've scanned all the ground.

First Semichorus
And discovered . . . ?

Second Semichorus
Labor enough; no trace of him we seek.

First Semichorus
Nor yet on the path to eastward, facing the sunrise:
No sign of him at all.

(The two halves of the Chorus unite.)

Chorus
What struggling fisherman
Of those that seek their haul
With labor in the hours of sleep;   880
What nymph of mountain side
Or seaward-rolling river
Might see the grim man
Wandering somewhere and cry out to me?
I wish one would! For surely
It's a hard thing that I must range and plod,
With never a fair course
To bring me near my goal;
But I cannot see the afflicted man's faint trace.   890

(Tecmessa has entered from the wing and reached the
place where Ajax has fallen. She is still invisible,
though, being masked by the bushes.)

Tecmessa

   Oh! No! No!

Chorus

   Whose is that harsh cry bursting from the copse?

Tecmessa

   Oh! Oh!

Chorus

   It is she, I see her now, the poor captive wife,
   Tecmessa. She is lost in lamentation.

Tecmessa

   Friends, I am ruined, overwhelmed, undone.

Chorus

   What is the matter?

Tecmessa

   Here at my feet lies Ajax, newly slain.
   His fallen body enfolds and hides the sword.

Chorus

   Oh, now I shall not win home!   900
   You have dealt me death, my lord,
   Your poor unhappy shipmate.
   —And I feel for her, poor wretched one, poor wife!

Tecmessa

   He is dead, dead. We can only weep for him.

Chorus

   Whose hand helped him to his fate?

Tecmessa

   His own hand and act. It's plain to see.
   This blade, packed in the ground,
   On which he fell, declares it.

Chorus

   How blind I was! And you bled alone, your friends not guarding!   910
   I was all deaf and stupid, totally heedless.

Let me see him,
Rugged and ill-starred Ajax, where he lies.

Tecmessa

You *must* not see him! I will cover him
With this enfolding garment from all sight.

> (*She removes her own mantle, which should be ample*
> *and rectangular, and covers him.*)

Surely no one who loved him could endure
To see the foam at his nostrils and the spout
Of darkening blood from the wound his own hand made.
Alas, what shall I do? Which of your friends   920
Will bear you up? Where's Teucer? Oh, may he come in time
To give fit tendance to his fallen brother!
Ajax! To be so great, and suffer this!
Even your enemies, I think, might weep for you.

Chorus

You were bound, hard spirit,
Bound in the end (it is clear now)
To work the term of your luckless
Life's share of affliction, that vast journey.
What could they mean but that,
The groans your fierce heart uttered
By night and in the sunlight,   930
Fraught with hate
For the sons of Atreus,
Fraught with a mind for harm?
That time was to be a great
Inaugural time of sorrows
When the strife was set for soldiership
Over the priceless armor.

Tecmessa

Oh! The pain of it!

Chorus

A noble grief, I know, goes to the heart.

Tecmessa
    Oh! Oh!

Chorus
    I don't wonder, lady,
    That you cry out, and again cry out, your grief,   940
    Deprived so recently of one so dear.

Tecmessa
    You may conjecture that;
    I know and feel it all too certainly.

Chorus
    That is true.

Tecmessa
    Poor little one! What a yoke of servitude
    We go to! What hard taskmasters!

Chorus
    They are ruthless indeed, the two sons of Atreus,
    If they do the unspeakable thing
    You have spoken in your distress:
    God forbid!

Tecmessa
    Even in what we suffer I see the gods' hand.   950

Chorus
    Yes, they have given an overload of grief.

Tecmessa
    I think Pallas, the dreadful goddess, has bred
    This pain, perhaps for her favorite, Odysseus.

Chorus
    That waiting, laboring man,
    How he insults in his black heart!
    He mocks our madding griefs
    With loud laughter, bitter to bear,
    And the twin kings hear and join him.   960

Tecmessa

Well, let them laugh their laughter and exult
In Ajax' downfall. They didn't want him living;
Perhaps, now he is dead, they will yearn for him,
When the fighting presses. Ignorant men
Don't know what good they hold in their hands until
They've flung it away. His death was a bitterer thing to me
Than sweet to them; but for himself a happiness.
For he won his great desire, the death he looked for.
Why should those others mock him any more?
His death concerns the gods, not them at all.   970
Let Odysseus think of this and make his empty insult.
For them there is no Ajax; mine is gone,
But not the grief and loss he leaves to me.

(Teucer is heard in the wing.)

Teucer

O God! God!

Chorus

Hush! For I think it's Teucer's voice I hear,
And his cry goes straight to the mark of this disaster.

(Teucer enters.)

Teucer

O my dear brother Ajax, have you come
To grief, as this strong rumor says you have?

Chorus

He is dead, Teucer. Know the simple truth.

Teucer

Then my ill-luck is bearing heavily down!   980

Chorus

It is true.

Teucer

       Miserable!

Chorus

  You may well groan.

Teucer

                  Rash and calamitous!

Chorus

  Yes, Teucer.

Teucer

              The grief comes sharp. But where
  Is the little one? Where in the whole width
  Of Troyland shall I look for him?

Chorus

                          He is alone

  By the tents.

Teucer (to Tecmessa)

  Go quickly, then,
  Quickly, and bring him here. Some enemy else
  May snatch him, as one would a lion-whelp
  Torn from its mother. Hurry and lose no time!
  When a man lies dead and cannot help himself,
  The world delights to mock and injure him.

                                    (*Exit Tecmessa.*)

Chorus

  Teucer, that was his last command to you,   990
  To take care for his child, as you are doing.

Teucer

  This sight of all sights that my eyes have seen
  To me is harshest, and no other road,
  Of all my feet have taken, so has grieved
  My soul as this, dear Ajax, which I took
  In haste to seek the truth and trace it home
  When first I heard the news of your disaster.
  It was sharp news, and sped through all the army
  As if some God had sent it: you were dead.
  And when I heard it, still a long way off,   1000

I groaned with inward misery; now I see;
It is true, and it destroys me.
Ah, me!
Come and uncover; let me see the worst.

(He uncovers the face of Ajax.)

Hard, bitter countenance, lines of fierce resolve,
How can I look at you? Oh, what a crop
Of anguish you have sown for me in death!
Where can I go? Who ever will receive me,
Now I have failed to help you in your need?
Old Telamon is your father, and mine too:
No doubt he'll welcome me and beam on me
When I come home without you. Very likely!   1010
He's not much given to smiling, even when things go well.
What will he not say? What reproach will he spare me?
Bastard and *gotten by the war-spear, coward,*
Nerveless deserter and *abandoner*—
Of you, dear Ajax! or perhaps suggest
I did it out of treachery, so that I
Might get your house and kingship by your death.
These will be that harsh old man's reproaches:
Age makes him morose and stirs him up
To causeless anger. In the end I'll be
Cast into exile and denied my country,
A slave in his account and not a freeman.   1020
At home those are my expectations; here in Troy
My enemies are numerous, my help small.
Such are the benefits your death has brought me.
What shall I do? How shall I disengage you,
Brother, from off this bitter, gleaming spike,
Your murderer, by whose cut you gasped your life out?
Do you see how in time Hector, though dead,
Was to destroy you? Only consider this
Amazing thing, the fortunes of two men:
The girdle Hector had as Ajax' gift
Was that which dragged him from the chariot rails,   1030

Clamping his flesh and grating him until
He swooned in death; this sword Hector gave Ajax,
Who perished on it with a death-fraught fall.
Did not a Fury beat this weapon out?
And was it not Aidoneus, that grim craftsman,
Who made that other one? In my opinion,
This was the gods' contrivance, like all other
Destinies of men, for the gods weave them all;
But if anyone should find my thought at fault,
Let him keep his opinion, and I mine.

Chorus

Cut short your speech, and quickly consider   1040
How best to hide him in some sort of grave,
And what you must say next. I see a man
Coming, our enemy, to laugh, I think,
Like one who means us harm, at our misfortunes.

Teucer

Which chief of the army is it that you see?

Chorus

Menelaus, the one we made this voyage to gratify.

Teucer

I see him now.
At closer range he's not hard to distinguish.

                    (Enter Menelaus, attended by two heralds.)

Menelaus

You, there! I tell you not to lift that corpse
Nor bury it, but leave it where it is.

Teucer

And why the expense of this somewhat grand announcement?

Menelaus

My pleasure, and the High Command's decree.   1050

Teucer

Perhaps you'd care to give some justification for it.

Menelaus

Listen, then.
When we brought Ajax here from Greece,
We thought he would be our ally and our friend:
On trial we've found him worse than any Trojan—
Plotting a murderous blow at the whole army,
A night attack, to nail us with his spear.
And unless some god had smothered that attempt,
We should have met the end that he has met,
Done to a helpless, miserable death,
And he be living still. But God changed   1060
His criminal heart to fall on sheep and cattle.
Therefore I say, no man exists on earth
Who shall have the power to give him burial,
But he shall be tossed forth
Somewhere on the pale sand, to feed the sea birds.
There it is, and I want no fire-breathing.
Maybe we couldn't rule him while he lived;
But now he is dead, we most assuredly will,
With a firm directing hand, whether you like it or not.
So long as he lived, he never would heed our words,   1070
Never. And yet it's a poor common soldier
That feels no duty to obey his betters.
Laws will never be rightly kept in a city
That knows no fear or reverence, and no army
Without its shield of fear can be well governed.
And even if a man rears a huge frame,
He had better know how small a cause can throw him.
When a man is moved by wholesome fear and shame,
You may know that combination makes for safety;   1080
But insubordination and the rule
Of do-as-you-like invariably, mark my words,
Sooner or later drive a city on
Before the gale into the sea's gulf.
Enact, I say, some salutary fear:
And let's not think we can do just what we please,

And then, when we grow vexatious, pay no fees.
There's turnabout in these things. A while ago
He was the hot aggressor; now it's I
Who entertain large ideas. And I give you notice,
Don't bury him. For you may find, if you do,
That you're apt to take a tombward fall yourself.   1090

Chorus

Menelaus, these are fine principles you've upreared;
Don't shame them now by outrage to the dead.

Teucer

Friends, I never shall be amazed again
To see a man of humble birth go wrong,
When those who claim the noblest birth of all
Utter such wrongful speech as you've just heard.
Come, tell me again: you say you brought this man
Here for the Greeks as an ally *you* enlisted?
Didn't he make the voyage here on his own,
As his own master? How, then, are you his general?   1100
What gives you title to command his people,
Who followed him from home? King of Sparta
You came, no general over us. You've no more claim
To marshal him than he has to drill you.
Why, you sailed here in a subordinate place,
Not lord of all, that you should ever claim
The right to captain Ajax! Rule your own;
Chastise their arrogant speech. But Ajax,
In spite of your prohibitions and your brother's,
I shall lay in his tomb, reverently and justly,
Regardless of your frowns. It wasn't at all   1110
For your wife's sake he made the expedition,
Like some poor, toiling subject; but for the oaths
Which he had sworn—no service due to you.
He took no stock of nobodies. Think this over,
And come then with more heralds at your back,

And maybe the general too. But I'll take no notice
Of your pother, so long as you're what you are.

Chorus

I can't approve such bold speech in misfortune;
Harsh words, however just they are, still rankle.

Menelaus

This bowman seems to think quite well of himself.   1120

Teucer

My archery is no contemptible science.

Menelaus

Think how he'd boast if he wore a warrior's armor!

Teucer

I'm a match light-armed for you in bronze, I think.

Menelaus

That tongue of yours! What a fierce heart it fosters!

Teucer

A man may have some boldness in the right.

Menelaus

So! It was right he should kill me and then prosper!

Teucer

Kill? Truly this *is* a miracle,
If you've been killed and still are living!

Menelaus

A god saved me; I was dead in *his* intention.

Teucer

Well, don't affront the gods, if the gods have saved you.

Menelaus

Could it be that I should fail to revere the gods' laws?   1130

Teucer

Yes, if you intervene
To interrupt the burial of the dead.

Menelaus

Of my own enemies! *They* must not be buried.

Teucer

Ajax opposed you, then, on the field of battle?

Menelaus

He hated me, as I did him. You knew that well.

Teucer

There was some reason for it:
You were found out procuring fraudulent votes.

Menelaus

Charge his defeat to the judges, not to me.

Teucer

You have a gift for suave and stealthy villainy.

Menelaus

Someone is going to smart for that speech.

Teucer

No worse, I judge, than the smart I shall inflict.

Menelaus

I tell you just one thing. This man must not be buried.   1140

Teucer

And this shall be your answer. He shall be
Buried at once.

Menelaus

I observed a man once of fast and saucy speech
Who had pressed sailors to make a voyage in a storm;
When the weather got really rough, you couldn't hear
Him piping anywhere: he hid himself in his cloak,
And anybody aboard could step on him at will.
And very possibly you and your reckless speech—
If a big whistling storm should suddenly come
Out of a little cloud—your clamorous uproar
Might be quenched in a very similar fashion.

Teucer

And I once saw a man inflated with foolishness,   1150
Who insulted the misfortunes of his neighbors.
And another man, closely resembling me,

Quite like me in temperament, gave him a straight look
And said to him, "Man, don't outrage the dead.
You certainly shall regret it if you do."
That was the advice he gave that worthless man.
I see him now, and he is, it seems to me,
You, and nobody else. Am I speaking in riddles?

Menelaus

I'm leaving. I shall only look absurd
To stay and chide you, when I might use force.   1160

(Exit.)

Teucer

Go, then. It does me little credit, either,
To listen to an empty man's loud talk.

Chorus

A great and wrathful contest is shaping.
Teucer, bestir yourself. Find him,
As quickly as you can, some hollow
Cavity in the earth, that shall become
His dank, capacious tomb, a signal
Reminder of him to men in after time.

Teucer

Here, just in time for that, his wife and child
Are coming, to perform with kindred touch
The service due his pitiable body.   1170

(Enter Tecmessa with Eurysaces.)

Come, little one, kneel down, as suppliants do,
Grasp your father, the creator of your life.
Hold in your hands this lock of mine

(Cuts it, and puts it in the boy's hand.)
and hers,

(Cuts it, etc.)

And this, a third, your own

(Puts his hand on the boy's head and separates the lock
in readiness to cut it.)

—a suppliant's treasure.
Keep your station, and make your supplication.
And if anyone in the army tries to wrest you
Forcibly from this corpse, may his corpse be
Thrown out unburied from his land and home,
Wretchedly, as he is a wretch, cut off
At the root with all his race, even as I
Have cut this lock of hair.

(Cuts it and gives it to Eurysaces.)

Take it, dear child, and guard it, and let no one   1180
Remove you, but cling fast, inclining over him.

(To the Chorus)

And you, don't huddle near like a crowd of women,
Instead of the men you are, but rally round
And help, till I come back, having provided
A tomb for him, though all the world gainsay me.

(Exit Teucer.)

Chorus
   Strophe
   Which year, I wonder, shall be my long toil's last,
   And when shall the battered count of them all be full?
   They bring upon me a ceaseless curse of spear-sped
   Trouble over the length and breadth of Troy,   1190
   A grief and a shame to all Greek men.

   Antistrophe
   Whoever it was that first revealed to Hellas
   Their common scourge, detested arms and war,
   I curse him. Would the large air first had taken him
   Or else the impartial house of Death. Generations
   Of toil be made for us. Ah,
   There indeed was a harrier of men!

   Strophe
   It was he that denied my share
   In the sweet companionship   1200

Of garland and deep cup;
And miserly he grudged me
The flute's soft lovely clamor
And a pleasant bed in the night,
And love, love he abridged and interdicted.
Ah, me! I languish, so. None cares
That my locks are damp with the thick continual dew
Which is all my thought of Troy.   1210

   Antistrophe
And he, valorous Ajax,
Who was once my ward and cover
From every flying shaft
And dread in the hours of night,
Now is handed over to his harsh daemon.
What joy, then, is left to me?
Oh, if somehow I might find myself
Rounding a wood-topped bulwark of the sea,
Sunium's level tip where the surf washes,
And make my salutation   1220
To holy Athens!

                              (*Enter Teucer hastily.*)

Teucer

   I hurried back when I saw the commander-in-chief,
   Agamemnon, approaching. And here he is;
   I think he will give his hateful lips full freedom.

                    (*Enter Agamemnon with retinue.*)

Agamemnon

   You, there! Are you the one they tell me of,
   Who has made bold to yawp these powerful speeches,
   Unpunished, so far, against me? You,
   The son of a captive slave-woman! What if your mother
   Had been a princess? *Then* I think you'd strut,   1230
   Then you'd talk big! Why, as it is, being
   Nothing yourself, you have risen up to protect
   That man who now is nothing, and have sworn
   That I am not the general nor the admiral

Either of the Achaeans or of you,
Since Ajax, as you say, came under his own command!
These are quite some taunts to hear from a slave.
And what is the man on whose behalf you've bawled
These very ambitious claims? Where did he go,
Or stand in battle, where I did not too?
Was he the one real man in the whole Greek army?   1240
Ah! that contest for Achilles' armor!
We shall regret the day we published it
If every moment we must be defamed
And slandered by this Teucer, if you please!
Who can't accept the court's majority verdict,
Defeated as he is, or yield to it,
No! but you losers pelt us still with slanders,
And seek to wound us with your crafty plots.
Yet where such reckless courses have their head,
No law can stand unshaken, not when we
Must shove the lawful victors from their place,
And give precedence to the ranks behind.
This must be curbed. It's not a man's great frame   1250
Or breadth of shoulders makes his manhood count:
A man of sense has always the advantage.
A very little whip can serve to guide
A hulking ox straight forward on his road.
And I fancy something of that medicine
Is coming for you, unless you get some sense!
That man is dead, now—just a shadow;
And yet you seem to count on *him* to protect
Your sauciness! I say, learn moderation!
Think of your slave's birth; bring someone else,   1260
A freeman, here to plead your case before me.
I'm disinclined to hear more words from you,
Being not much versed in your barbarian speech.

Chorus

I wish you both might learn a moderate mind!
That is the best I have to say to you.

Teucer

    Alas! How fugitive is the gratitude
    Men owe the dead, how soon shown to deceive!
    This man has no trifling remembrance,
    Ajax, of you, though oftentimes for him
    You risked your life and bore the stress of war.
    All that is gone now, easily tossed away.
    You, who just now spoke that long, foolish speech,
    Can't you remember any more at all
    How you were penned once close behind your picket,
    And all but ruined in the rout of war   1270
    With flames licking the ships' quarter-decks
    Already, and Hector high in the air, leaping
    Over the fosse to board, but Ajax came,
    Alone, to save you? Who fended off *that* ruin?
    Wasn't it he, the very man you now   1280
    Declare fought nowhere but where you fought too?
    What do you say? Did he deal fairly then?
    And when that other time he closed alone
    In single fight with Hector, not conscripted,
    But chosen when each champion put his lot
    Into the crested helmet—Ajax then
    Put in no shirking lot among the rest,
    No clod of moist earth, no! but one to skip
    Lightly, first and victorious, from the helm.
    It was he that did those things, and I stood by him:
    The slave, yes! the barbarian mother's son!
    Wretched man, why do you light upon *that* taunt?   1290
    Aren't you aware that your own grandfather,
    Old Pelops, was a barbarous Phrygian? Or
    That Atreus, yes, your actual *father*, set
    Before his brother a most unholy dish
    Of his own sons' flesh? And you yourself
    Had a Cretan for your mother, in whose bed
    An interloping foreigner was discovered,
    And she consigned, and by her parent's order,

To drown among the fishes of the deep.
These are your origins. Can you censure mine?
Telamon was my father, and he won
My mother as his valorous prize of war.   1300
She was a princess by her birth, the child
Of King Laomedon, and Heracles
Distinguished her to be my father's gift.
Two royal races gave me to the world.
How shall I shame my kin if I defend them
In their adversity, when you with shameless words
Would fling them out unburied? Listen to this:
If you should venture to cast Ajax out,
You must cast out the three of us as well,
Together in one heap with him. I make my choice
To stand in public and to die for him,   1310
Rather than for your wife—or was it your brother's wife?
So! Think of your own case, and not merely mine;
For if you vex me, you may wish you had been
A coward, rather than too bold with me.

(*Enter Odysseus.*)

Chorus

You arrive, my lord Odysseus, just in time,
If you have come to make not strife but peace.

Odysseus

What is this, gentlemen? For quite some distance
I could hear the sons of Atreus raising their voices
Over this valiant corpse.

Agamemnon

Indeed we were.
Hadn't we just been hearing infamous language,   1320
My lord Odysseus, from this fellow here?

Odysseus

What language do you complain of? If he gave
Insult for insult, I could pardon him.

Agamemnon

    I gave him ugly words:
    It was an ugly wrong he offered me.

Odysseus

    What did he do to injure you?

Agamemnon

                   He said
    He would not leave that corpse unburied, but
    Declared he'd bury it in spite of me.

Odysseus

    Agamemnon, may a friend speak truth to you,
    And still enjoy your friendship as before?

Agamemnon

    Speak. I would be foolish to resent your words;   1330
    You are my truest friend in the whole army.

Odysseus

    Then listen. Don't cast out this brave man's body
    Unburied; don't in the gods' name be so hard.
    Vindictiveness should not so govern you
    As to make you trample on the right. I too
    Found this man hateful once, beyond the rest
    Of all my fellow soldiers, since the time
    I won Achilles' armor. Nevertheless,
    In spite of his enmity, I cannot wish
    To pay him with dishonor, or refuse
    To recognize in him the bravest man   1340
    Of all that came to Troy, except Achilles.
    It would be wrong to do him injury;
    In acting so, you'd not be injuring him—
    Rather the gods' laws. It's a foul thing to hurt
    A valiant man in death, though he *was* your enemy.

Agamemnon

    Do you, Odysseus, take his part against me?

Odysseus
    I do.
    I hated him while it was fair to hate.

Agamemnon
    But now he is dead,
    Shouldn't you rightly trample on his corpse?

Odysseus
    Forbear, my lord, to seek unworthy triumphs.

Agamemnon
    Reverence doesn't come easily to a prince.   1350

Odysseus
    Regard for a friend's advice is not so difficult.

Agamemnon
    A good man should defer to his superiors.

Odysseus
    No more, now.
    You win the victory when you yield to friends.

Agamemnon
    Think what a man you're interceding for!

Odysseus
    My enemy, it's true. But he was noble.

Agamemnon
    Do you intend pity to a corpse you hate?

Odysseus
    His greatness weighs more than my hate with me.

Agamemnon
    Men who act so are changeable and unsteady.

Odysseus
    Men's minds are given to change in hate and friendship.

Agamemnon
    Do you, then, recommend such changeable friends?   1360

Odysseus

    I cannot recommend a rigid spirit.

Agamemnon

    You'll make me look a coward in this transaction.

Odysseus

    Generous, though, as all the Greeks will say.

Agamemnon

    You want me, then, to let this corpse be buried?

Odysseus

    Yes. For I too shall come to that necessity.

Agamemnon

    In everything, I see, men labor for themselves.

Odysseus

    For whom should I rather labor than myself?

Agamemnon

    Let this be called your doing, and not mine.

Odysseus

    However you do it, you will deserve praise.

Agamemnon

    Understand my position. I would do   1370
    This and much more at your request. But as for him,
    Whether on earth or in the underworld,
    I hate him. You may do whatever you wish.

                    (*Exit Agamemnon with his retinue.*)

Chorus

    Whoever fails to recognize your wisdom
    And value it, Odysseus, is a fool.

Odysseus

    And now I have a promise,
    Teucer, to make to you. From now on, I
    Shall be as much your friend as I was once
    Your enemy; and I should like to join

In the burial of your dead—doing with you
That labor, and omitting none of it,
Which men should give the noblest of their fellows. 1380

Teucer

Noble Odysseus, I can only praise you.
How greatly you deceived my expectations!
For though you hated him worst of the Argives,
You alone came to help, and did not wish,
Because you lived, to outrage him in death.
That wit-struck general did otherwise—
He and his noxious brother—and decreed
That Ajax' corpse should rot without a tomb.
Therefore, may Zeus who rules on high Olympus,
Remembering Furies, and avenging Justice 1390
Destroy them miserably, just as they
Sought to work outrage and abomination
On my dear brother's body. Son of Laertes,
I feel some hesitation at your offer
And fear I cannot let you touch the corpse:
That might offend the dead. But bear your part
In all the rest, and if you wish to bring
Any others of the army, they shall be welcome.
I'll see to all the rest. But you, Odysseus,
Are written in our hearts a nobleman.

Odysseus

I could have wished to help. 1400
But if your preference is otherwise,
I shall respect your wish and take my leave.

(*Exit Odysseus.*)

Teucer

Shoulder the work. Delay
Has grown too long already.
Some of you hurry and dig
The hollow trench; others
Set the tall cauldron

Amid the surrounding flames
To ready the holy bath;
And one troop bring from within the tent
His glorious suit of armor.

Now you, my boy,
Take hold with your little strength   1410
Upon your father's body,
And help in tenderness to lift him up;
For still the warm conduits
Spout forth his life's dark force.
Come now, come, everyone
That claims to be his friend,
Begin, proceed, and bear him up,
This man of perfect excellence—
No nobler one has ever been than he:
I speak of Ajax, while he lived.

(The cortege forms.)

Chorus
What men have seen they know;
But what shall come hereafter
No man before the event can see,
Nor what end waits for him.   1420

(Exeunt, following the body.)

THE WOMEN OF TRACHIS

Translated by Michael Jameson

INTRODUCTION TO *THE WOMEN*
OF TRACHIS

Heracles was rarely the subject of tragedy, although the most popular hero of Greek mythology. In the theater he was more commonly seen in satyr plays and comedy, and, indeed, this is an indication of his great appeal: he was both god and man, hero and buffoon. At times he appeared as a rescuer to conclude a play in which he was not the central character (in Aeschylus' lost *Prometheus Unbound*, in Euripides' *Alcestis*, in Sophocles' *Philoctetes*), but he is not tragic at such times or in the triumphant accomplishment of his labors but at the moment of his solitary defeat. Sophocles and Euripides (in his *Heracles*) each took for his plot one of his two defeats, while ignoring the other—his agony in the poisoned shirt and his homicidal madness against his wife and children. It may be that a single, terrible defeat is necessary to the career of one who is Everyman on a heroic scale and that the poisoned shirt and the madness are "doublets," coming from different versions of his life, concerning two different wives who are only later combined into a single account. Modern research suggests that at least two heroes have merged to form the classical Heracles—the one from Tiryns, the other from Thebes.

Our play contains the first sure reference to Heracles' decision to be burned alive on the pyre, although two divergent traditions about his end are as early as Homer and Hesiod: the one, that, great as he was, even the son of Zeus had to die like any other man; the other, that, after battling Death in various guises, he wins immortality among the gods on Olympus. In later times this latter is the dominant version, and the pyre which destroys his mortal body is the means of his ascent, as in Seneca's *Hercules Oetaeus*. The story of the pyre cannot be original with Sophocles, for we see it on Attic vases beginning in the early part of the century, and it seems always to have been connected with his becoming a god. Why, then, does

Sophocles avoid all reference to the final resolution of the hero's agony? For Heracles here expects death, and there is not the slightest hint of apotheosis, although it is explicit in the poet's *Philoctetes*. To find an answer, we must see the place of the last scene in the play, assuming that it is an integral part of the whole and not a conventional appendage dictated by mythology.

At the beginning Deianira tells us: "Now he wins through to the end of all his labors / and now I am more than ever afraid" (ll. 36–37), and soon after she reports a prophecy to her son Hyllus: "It said that either he would come to his life's end / or have by now, and for the rest of his time, / a happy life, once he had carried out this task" (ll. 79–81). So the play begins with his wife's anxiety over Heracles' last labors, which will mean the "end" (*telos*) for him and for her, in all its ambiguity; and it is the working-out of this end through a series of revelations constantly coming closer to the full truth that is the action of the play. When Heracles realizes that his end has come and has added further strokes to complete his fate, he closes the action with the order that he be carried out to the pyre to be burned alive: "The true / respite from suffering is this—my final end" (ll. 1255–56). It is this, the discovery of the end of Heracles, that gives the play its unity; for clearly, as the action is not centered on a single character, it does not have the obvious unity of an *Oedipus the King*, nor can it be made into such a play by ignoring either Heracles or Deianira and regarding the remaining character as the true hero. The title we have, avoiding both the principals, should be a warning. And once we allow that the subject of the play is larger than the tragedy of either character and inextricably involves both, we cannot stop short of the total action; to see the play, for instance, as an exposition of the destructive power of love makes a mere "afterpiece" of the last scene, where Heracles learns the truth and acts upon it. Rather, this is the play's climax as well as its conclusion.

The movement of the play as a series of revelations is expressed in action and imagery and is underscored in language through the prominent use in the Greek of the root of *phainein* ("reveal") and of its synonyms and opposites (there is a similar emphasis on *telos*, "end," and its derivatives). In imagery the contrast of the dark, secret, night-time, and deadly with the bright and clear, with sun, fire, and lightning, culminates in the black, dead enemies (the Hydra's poison, Nessus' gift) that defeat Heracles, and the fire with which in turn he will vanquish them and himself. In action, the expected appearance of Heracles, seemingly assured, is replaced by the silent mystery of Iole and the concealment of Lichas, which, when exposed, are followed by the secrecy of Deianira and of Nessus, revealed to Deianira by the sunlight on the tuft of wool, to the world by the altar fire at Cenaeum; the full revelation of his end to Heracles and of his further decision coincides with a new discovery— the revelation of Hyllus' character as a son worthy of his father.

There is also revelation of the divine agency behind the events: Lichas calls his false story of why Heracles has been absent so long "a tale where it is seen Zeus did the work" (l. 251, *praktōr phanei*); later, when the truth is out, "that silent / handmaiden, Cyprian Aphrodite / is revealed; this is her work" (ll. 859–61, *phanera . . . ephanē praktōr*); but in the end, when all is seen to agree with Zeus's oracles, "there is / nothing here which is not Zeus" (ll. 1277–78). Through the oracles mentioned at the beginning and near the end, we see that the events leading up to Heracles' defeat are part of the external, inevitable pattern against which the suffering and the actions of the characters must be seen. What happens when Heracles understands this pattern, being in accord with it and yet beyond it, may be the most important part of the play. As far as the characters, or we, can see, the Gods do not care. The meaning and worth of men's actions are what they make of them. We may remember now that "Sophocles claimed he depicted men as they ought to be, Euripides as they are" (Aristotle *Poetics* xxv. 11). If Euripides' characters were closer to reality, Sophocles' own were larger than life, on a heroic scale. How do his characters here fit his own description?

Deianira is easily the more sympathetic character for the modern reader, and many have been tempted to read the play as her tragedy. We see in the beginning her early fear of marriage and of lust, symbolized for her by the monstrous Acheloüs and then by Nessus; strictly outside the action, they are kept before us by her own and the

chorus' reminiscence. For the end of Heracles' toils means her husband at rest at home and the end of violence and fear. No sooner has
all this been realized, as it seems, than violence and lust burst into
her own house and her own bed. Here we first see her stature in her
kindness and her restraint after she knows who Iole is, in her refusal
to hurt or even blame her husband or the girl. (Throughout there
may well be a contrast intended with Aeschylus' Clytemnestra in the
Agamemnon.) She resorts to a love charm with reluctance and misgiv-
ings, for they were unbecoming a great lady and notoriously dangerous. We feel that she was incredibly foolish to trust a gift from
Nessus, and soon she thinks so too, and yet we may fail to appreciate
how plausible is his magic: the blood of Nessus is to her vile and
repulsive, no less so because of the vaguely apprehended effect of the
Hydra's poison, but it is precisely from the vile and repulsive that the
most potent magic comes. Furthermore, Nessus and the centaurs in
general were an incarnation of the erotic (as his attempt on her con-
firms—the poet's taste seems to have suppressed a peculiarly appropriate ingredient of the charm found in the tradition, the centaur's
semen). What better source for a love charm to turn back toward his
wife the lust of Heracles, "all desire when the beast's / inducements,
all dipped in persuasion, have melted him" (ll. 661–62)? When she is
told of the deadly effect of the poison and is cursed by her son, she
leaves without a word to justify herself and, re-enacting the central
ritual of her life, she makes the bed of Heracles for the last time and
kills herself upon it. "How could any woman bring her hands to
this?" (l. 898) the Chorus asks, for this is not the hanging of Jocasta
or Antigone but the more masculine self-destruction with the sword.
A woman, ordinary in her devotion to her marriage and family,
shows her extraordinary nobility and strength at the time of her
utter disaster.

But, for the Greeks, Heracles has even more of the heroic proper-
ties. No man has done more or suffered more. This is not to say that
he is likable or, in the sickness of his passion, admirable. Nonetheless,
for Deianira and Hyllus, when they think of her losing such a husband, he is "the best of all men" (ll. 177, 811–12). There is no idea of
his being punished for his immorality, nor is there any attempt to

soften the impact of his enormous faults. Everything about him is larger than life. When his violent lust is revealed, it is not treated as showing him to be any less of a hero but as evidence of the super-human power of the one foe that has overcome him. Love is seen as a sickness, and the poison, intended as a drug, a remedy, brings about another sickness that can be cured only by suicidal fire. "I ask you to be my healer, / the only physician who can cure my suffer-ing," he begs his son (ll. 1208-9). But this last sickness, the working of the poison, is also conceived of as a beast, the last of all that he has faced (cf. ll. 987, 1009 f., 1028 ff., 1053 ff.), and in the poet's language the other beasts are linked together to form a composite enemy that gains its late revenge. In this play, Heracles is more the beast-slayer than the savior of mankind, and it is in this role that, before he knows the truth, he thinks to punish Deianira. There is no point in reprov-ing him in his ignorance and his horrible pain for this desire. Is any other reaction conceivable for one who knows only what he knows, who is in his pain, and, most important, has led his life? ". . . alive / I punished the evil and I punish them in death" (ll. 1110-11). Nor need we reprove or gloss over his failure to forgive her when he knows she was innocent. The knowledge that the poison came from Nessus puts everything in a new light. Before, though he prayed for death, he had not, it would seem, admitted to himself that his end had come. Now he knows, and he turns to face it. His end is not to be avoided, but his agony remains, and he treats it as a sickness and as a beast. He had said that this "flowering of madness" was "inexorable" (akēlēton, l. 999, that is, "not to be charmed away"). "Is there any singer of spells, / any craftsman surgeon who can / exorcise this curse, but Zeus?" (ll. 1000-1002). Now, calmly, forcing his will on his son, he applies the measures he had called for in his delirium: the fire and the sword he had used in his purification, purging the earth of beasts (ll. 1013 ff.), he turns on himself, resuming the role he has played all his life.

One cannot doubt that the audience as a whole would have thought beyond to the apotheosis, but, by suppressing all mention of elevation to the Gods through fire and by not motivating the fire through an oracle, the poet focuses attention on the thing chosen—the fire itself as destroying and purifying—and on the act of choosing. Heracles suffers and acts not with the promise of immortality but with the firm expectation of death, and it is this which gives meaning to his choice. The hero who has wept and wailed, shamefully vanquished by a woman and his dead enemies, returns to the attack, even as Oedipus puts out his eyes, Ajax yields, only to choose suicide, and Antigone, buried alive, kills herself. Heracles tells his "tough soul," ". . . make an end / of this unwanted, welcome task" (ll. 1259 ff.). He makes his end his own.

Appropriately, it is Hyllus who closes the play, for it is through him that we have felt the emotional impact of the long last scene—Heracles, however stunning his actions, is hardly enough like us now for sympathy. When Hyllus accused his mother, we wanted to cry out, "She did not mean to . . ." and almost at once, with her death, his contrition acknowledges, as it were, that we were right. Now the new blows are felt through our sympathy with him. He must restrain his half-crazed father in his ghastly agony, he must brave a murderous anger to tell him the truth, and he must burn, or all but burn, his father alive and marry the woman he thinks of as his parents' murderer. The dramatic power of the scene needs no comment, but we should also see that thus he ends the chain of violent love by accepting a marriage that appalls him, assuming his father's mantle where alone his father had not triumphed through courage and endurance.

Finally, what of Zeus and the Gods who have shown so little compassion in "all that's happened; they / who are called our fathers, who begot us, / can look upon such suffering" (ll. 1266–69)? For Sophocles, in this play at least, the Gods are "the way things are"—the invincible power of love, the predicted and inevitable end; they form the immovable background to human suffering and heroism. The action of the play insists that this is so, that there is what we might call an "inhuman" design, but it is more concerned with what, this being so, Deianira, Heracles, and Hyllus do and suffer and with the way in which, whatever their weakness, they show how men ought to be.

The Date

The date of the play is not known. Internal evidence has led to widely different conclusions, but a comparison with certain features of Euripides' *Medea* (431 B.C.) and *Heracles* (420–419 B.C.?) seems to help in placing it in the twenties of the fifth century. The date is of interest primarily for the study of Sophocles' development and for possible relations with the work of Euripides. The play is utterly apolitical. It was, then, probably written after *Ajax* and *Antigone*, close to *Oedipus the King*, when the poet was past sixty, and with *Electra* (probably) and *Philoctetes* and *Oedipus at Colonus* certainly still to come.

A Note on the Text

For the most part I have translated the text of A. C. Pearson ("Oxford Classical Texts" [Oxford, 1923]); at a few points I have agreed with R. C. Jebb (*The Trachiniae*, Part V of *Sophocles, The Plays and Fragments* [Cambridge, 1892]) as against Pearson, especially in lines 207, 328, 526, 660, 837, 905, 1084, 1186, and 1191; more rarely I have departed from the interpretation of a word or phrase preferred by Jebb in his commentary, especially in lines 35, 101, 216, 231, 250, 309, 886, and 1010. In lines 100–102 the "sea-narrows" probably refer to the Bosphorus and Hellespont, the "twin continents" to Europe and Africa at the Pillars of Heracles (Gibraltar); this agrees with H. Lloyd-Jones, *Classical Quarterly*, XLVIII (1954), 91–92. Finally, with Wilamowitz, I add τέλος in line 528, and at line 857 I read Herwerden's ἅ τ᾽ὀλεθρίαν for τότε θοάν. I do not attempt any justification, since this is not the place and since, in any case, the choices have been much influenced by the exigencies of making a translation.

THE WOMEN OF TRACHIS

Deianira, *Wife of Heracles*

Nurse

Hyllus, *Son of Heracles and Deianira*

Chorus, *Women of Trachis, Friends of Deianira*

A Messenger

Lichas, *Herald of Heracles*

Captive Women of Oechalia, *Including the Young Iole (all silent parts)*

An Old Man

Heracles

Bearers and Attendants of Heracles *(silent parts)*

THE WOMEN OF TRACHIS

SCENE: *Trachis, before the house of Heracles and Deianira. Deianira and the Nurse enter from the house.*

Deianira

It was long ago that someone first said:
You cannot know a man's life before the man
has died, then only can you call it good or bad.
But I know mine before I've come to Death's house
and I can tell that mine is heavy and sorrowful.   5
While I still lived in Pleuron, with Oeneus my father,
I conceived an agonizing fear of marriage.
No other Aetolian woman ever felt such fear,
for my suitor was the river Acheloüs,
who used to come to ask my father for my hand,   10
taking three forms—first, clearly a bull, and then
a serpent with shimmering coils, then a man's body
but a bull's face, and from his clump of beard
whole torrents of water splashed like a fountain.
I had to think this suitor would be my husband   15
and in my unhappiness I constantly prayed for death
before I should ever come to *his* marriage bed.

But, after a time, to my joy there came
the famous Heracles, son of Alcmena and Zeus.
In close combat with Acheloüs, he won the contest   20
and set me free. I do not speak of the manner
of their struggles, for I do not know. Someone
who watched the spectacle unafraid could tell.
I sank down, overwhelmed with terror lest
my beauty should somehow bring me pain. Zeus of the contests   25
made the end good—if it has been good.

Chosen partner for the bed of Heracles,
I nurse fear after fear, always worrying
over him. I have a constant relay of troubles;
some each night dispels—each night brings others on.   30
We have had children now, whom he sees at times,
like a farmer working an outlying field,
who sees it only when he sows and when he reaps.
This has been his life, that only brings him home
to send him out again, to serve some man or other.   35

Now he wins through to the end of all his labors,
and now I find I am more than ever afraid.
Ever since he killed the mighty Iphitus,
we, his family, live here in Trachis, a stranger's guests,
forced to leave our home. But no one seems to know   40
where Heracles himself can be. I only know
he's gone and left with me a sharp pain for him.
I am almost sure that he is in some trouble.
It has not been a short time—first a year,
by now still more, and there has been no word of him.   45
Yes, this tablet he left behind makes me think
it must surely be some terrible trouble. Often
I pray the Gods I do not have it for my sorrow,

Nurse

Deianira, my mistress, many times before
I have watched as you wept and sobbed, bewailing   50
your absent Heracles, and I said nothing. But now
I wonder—if it is proper that the free should learn
from the thoughts of slaves and I give you advice—
how is it that your family abounds with sons, and yet
you send no one to inquire for your husband?   55
Hyllus, especially, it would be natural to send
if he is at all concerned for his father's safety.
See, here he is, running to the house,
so if what I have said seems of any value,
you can use the boy and follow my advice.   60

(*Hyllus enters from the wings.*)

Deianira

O my child, my son, even the low-born throw
a lucky cast when they speak well. This woman is
a slave, but what she says is worthy of the free.

Hyllus

What is it she said? Tell me, Mother, if you may.

Deianira

With your father abroad so long, it does not   65
look well that you have made no inquiry for him.

Hyllus

But I know where he is, if I can believe what I hear.

Deianira

My child, have you heard in what country he stays?

Hyllus

All this past year, in all its length of time
they say he was in service to a Lydian woman.   70

Deianira

If he could really endure that, then anything
might be said of him.

Hyllus

      He is free now, I hear.

Deianira

Then where is he now? Is he alive or dead?

Hyllus

They say he is in Euboea, where he campaigns against
the city of Eurytus, unless he is still preparing.   75

Deianira

Did you know, my child, that it was about
this very place he left me a true prophecy?

Hyllus

What prophecy, Mother? I knew nothing about this.

Deianira

It said that either he would come to his life's end
or have by now, and for the rest of his time,   80
a happy life, once he had carried out this task.
Child, his future lies in the balance. Surely, then,
you will go to help him, since we are only safe   83
if he can save himself. His ruin is ours.   85

Hyllus

I shall go, Mother, and had I known the contents
of this oracle before, I would have been there
long ago. As it was, my father's usual
good luck kept me from worrying and being too fearful.
Now that I know of it, I shall not stop until   90
I have learned the whole truth about his fate.

Deianira

Go now, my son. There is always some advantage
in learning good news, even if one learns it late.

> (*Hyllus leaves by one of the side entrances; the Chorus
> enters, speaking, by the other.*)

Chorus

Shimmering night as she lies despoiled brings you
to birth at dawn, lays you to bed ablaze—   95
O Sun, Sun! I beg you,
tell me of Alcmena's child.
Where, where is Heracles?
All afire with the brilliance of lightning, tell me!
—is he in the sea-narrows,   100
or does he rest against the twin
continents? Your sight is the strongest.

With longing in her heart for him, I learn
that Deianira, over whom men fought,
like some unhappy bird,   105
never lays to bed her longing,
her eyes tearless, but
nurses fear that well remembers her husband's

journey, worn upon her troubled
husbandless bed, miserable,   110
with expectation of misfortune.

As many waves under
the untiring south wind or north
may be seen on the wide
ocean coming on   115
and going by, so he, the descendant
of Cadmus is twisted, but on life's
next toilsome surge, as on the Cretan
deep, he will be elevated.
Some god always pulls him   120
safely back from the house of Death.

(The Chorus turns toward Deianira.)

Therefore, I reprove you,
respectfully, but still
dissenting. You should not let
all expectation of good   125
be worn away. Nothing painless
has the all-accomplishing King
dispensed for mortal men. But
grief and joy come circling
to all, like the turning paths   130
of the Bear among the stars.

The shimmering night does not stay
for men, nor does calamity,
nor wealth, but swiftly they are gone,
and to another man it comes
to know joy and its loss.   135
Therefore, I bid even you, O Queen, always
hold fast to this knowledge in your expectations.
When has Zeus been so careless of his children?   140

(Deianira comes forward and speaks.)

Deianira
    You are here, I suppose, because you have heard

of my suffering. May you never learn
by your own suffering how my heart is torn.
You do not know now. So the young thing
grows in her own places; the heat of the sun-god   145
does not confound her, nor does the rain, nor any wind.
Pleasurably she enjoys an untroubled life
until the time she is no longer called a maiden
but woman, and takes her share of worry in the night,
fearful for her husband or for her children. Then,   150
by looking at her own experience, she comes
to understand the troubles with which I am weighed down.

Many sufferings have made me weep before.
But I shall tell you of one unlike all the rest.
When King Heracles set off from home on his   155
last journey, he left an old tablet in the house,
on which some signs had been inscribed. Never before
could he bring himself to speak to me of this,
though he went out to many contests; he used to go
as if for some great achievement, not to die.   160
This once, as though he were no longer living, he told me
what property from our marriage I should take and how
he wished the portions of ancestral land divided
among the children, first fixing the time at three months
after he had been away from here one year: 165
then he would either die exactly at this time,
or, by getting past this time limit, he would
in the future live a life without grief.
He said that this was fated by the Gods to be
the final limit of the labors of Heracles,   170
as once at Dodona he heard the ancient oak
declare on the lips of the twin Doves, the priestesses.
The period of their prediction exactly coincides
with the present time, when all must come true;
so that I leap up from pleasant sleep in fright,   175
my friends, terrified to think that I may have to live
deprived of the one man who is the finest of all.

Chorus

Peace—speak words of good omen. I see a man
with laurel on his head who comes to speak to you.

> (*A messenger enters from the side in a great hurry,*
> *full of his important news.*)

Messenger

O Deianira, my mistress, I am the first messenger   180
to free you from your uncertainty. You should know
that Alcmena's son lives and is victorious
and brings from battle first-fruits for the gods of the land.

Deianira

What did you say, old man? What are you telling me?

Messenger

Soon there shall come to your halls that most enviable man,   185
your husband, appearing in his conquering might.

Deianira

Who told you this? Some townsman or a stranger?

Messenger

This is what Lichas, the herald, proclaims to many
in the meadow where the cattle pasture. I heard him
and rushed off, that, as the first to bring the news, I might   190
profit from your gratitude and gain your favor.

Deianira

Why is he not here himself if all is well?

Messenger

He is not free to move as he would like, lady.
Around him in a circle stand all the people of Malis
and question him. He is not able to take a step.   195
Everyone is curious and wants to know all
and will not let him go until he's heard him to
his heart's content. So though *he* does not want to, he stays
with those who want him. You will see him soon in person.

Deianira

O Zeus, master of the unharvested meadow of Oeta,   200
though it has been long, you have given us joy.

Cry out, O you women who are within the house
and you who are without—now that the unhoped-for sunshine
of this news has risen high, we pluck its gladness.

Chorus

Let there be joyous shouting for this house and jubilation   205
around the hearth by girls whose wedding is to come; and let the
    clamor
of men among them go in chorus to honor Apollo,
who wears the fine quiver, our defender. Together
raise on high the paean, paean, O maidens,   210
and shout aloud the name of his sister,
Artemis Ortygia, deer-hunter, who holds the twin torches,
and of the nymphs our neighbors.   215
I take it up, I shall not
push the flute aside, you master of my heart.
See how it excites me—
Euoi!—
the ivy that lately set the bacchants whirling in rivalry.   220
Oh, Oh, Paean! See, see, dear lady,
you are face to face with it now,
it is clear to look upon.

*(Enter Lichas, Heracles' envoy, followed by a group
of captive women, among them Iole.)*

Deianira

I do see the group that comes to us, dear women.   225
The sight did not slip past my sentinel eyes.
I proclaim our welcome to the herald, here after
a long time—if the news he brings is welcome.

Lichas

Our coming *is* good, lady, and good, too, our message,
based on accomplished fact. When a man prospers,   230
his profit must be to earn an excellent report.

Deianira

O kindest of men, tell me first what I want first
to hear: Shall I have Heracles alive?

Lichas

    I can tell you that I left him not only alive
    but strong and flourishing and unburdened by disease.   235

Deianira

    Where? In a Greek or in a foreign land? Tell me.

Lichas

    On a shore of Euboea, where he marks out altars
    and tributes of the land's harvest for Cenaean Zeus.

Deianira

    Is he fulfilling a vow or obeying an oracle?

Lichas

    A vow he took while he tried with his spear to overthrow   240
    the country of these women whom you see before you.

Deianira

    And by the gods, who are they, and who is their master?
    They are pitiable, if their misfortune does not deceive me.

Lichas

    He selected them when he sacked the city of Eurytus
    as possessions for himself and a choice gift for the Gods.   245

Deianira

    Was it against this city, then, that he was gone
    an unforeseeable time, days beyond number?

Lichas

    No, most of this time he was kept in Lydia,
    and, as he himself declares, he was not free
    but a bought slave. (One should not hesitate, lady,   250
    to tell a tale where it is seen Zeus did the work.)
    He was sold to Omphale, the foreign queen,
    and served her a full year, as he says himself,
    and was so stung by this disgrace he had to bear
    that he set himself an oath and swore that he   255
    would live to see the author of his suffering,
    along with wife and child, all in slavery.

These were not empty words, but when he was pure again,
he raised an army of strangers and came against the city
of Eurytus, who alone of mortals was   260
responsible, he claimed, for what he had suffered.
Heracles had come to his house and to his hearth
as an old friend. But Eurytus thundered greatly against him
like the sea and spoke with great malice in his heart:
Let Heracles have in his hands, he said, inescapable arrows.   265
In the bow's test *his* sons left Heracles behind,
as for speech—Heracles was a free man's slave,
a broken thing! Then he got him drunk at the banquet
and threw him out of the house. It was this that galled;
and when one day Iphitus came to the hill of Tiryns,   270
searching for the tracks of horses that had strayed,
the moment his eyes looked one way, his mind on something else,
Heracles hurled him from the top of that flat bastion.
But the King was angry at this act of his,
he who is the father of all, Zeus Olympian,   275
and had him sold and sent out of the country and did not relent,
since this was the only man he had ever killed
by guile. If he had taken vengeance openly,
Zeus surely would have pardoned his rightful victory.
The Gods like foul play no better than do men.   280
They who were so arrogant with their vicious tongues,
they themselves all are inhabitants of Hell,
while their city is enslaved. The women you see
come to you, finding, in place of prosperity,
an unenviable existence. These were your husband's wishes   285
which he commanded and I, faithful to him, fulfil.
You may be sure that he himself will come as soon
as he has made the holy sacrifice to Zeus,
God of his fathers, for his conquest. Of much news
happily reported, this must be the sweetest to hear.   290

Chorus

O Queen, now your delight is clear, both for what
has come about already, and what you have heard promised.

Deianira

    Yes, I should have every right to rejoice
    when I hear the news of my husband's great success.
    Surely my joy must keep pace with his good fortune.   295
    Still, if one gives it much thought, one knows a feeling
    of dread for the man who prospers so, lest he fall.
    For a terrible sense of pity came over me,
    my friends, when I saw these ill-fated women
    wandering homeless, fatherless, in a foreign land.   300
    Before they were, perhaps, the daughters of free men,
    but now they shall have to pass their lives as slaves.

    O Zeus, who turns the tide of battle, grant that I
    may never see you come like this against *my* children,
    and if you will come, at least not while I am alive.   305
    This is the fear I feel when I look at them.

                        (Deianira comes close to Iole.)
    O unfortunate girl, tell me who you are.
    Are you married? Are you a mother? To judge by your looks,
    you have never known treatment like this, but you
    are someone noble. Lichas, whose daughter is this girl?   310
    Who was her mother, and who was the father that begat her?
    Speak out, for on seeing her I pitied her most
    among these women, since only she knows how to feel.

Lichas

    What do *I* know? Why do you question me? Perhaps
    in birth she is not among the humblest of that land.   315

Deianira

    Not of royal birth? Had Eurytus a daughter?

Lichas

    I do not know. I made no long interrogation.

Deianira

    Did you not learn her name from one of her companions?

Lichas

    No, I did not. I performed my task in silence.

Deianira

Then do tell us yourself, my poor child, for it   320
would be a great shame not to know who *you* are.

Lichas

It will be quite unlike her manner up to now
if she begins to speak, I can assure you, since
she has not said a single thing, not one word yet.
She suffers constantly the weight of her misfortune   325
like pangs of labor, weeping and miserable, from the time
she left her wind-blown fatherland. Truly, it is her
bad luck that she cannot speak, but pardon her.

Deianira

Then let her be, and let her go into the house
however she please. She should not have further grief   330
on my account to add to her present unhappiness.
What she has already is enough. Let us all
enter the house so you may hasten wherever you wish
to go and I may see to the preparations within.

> (*Deianira turns to lead Lichas and the captive women into the
> house; the Messenger, who had stayed to one side while
> Lichas spoke with Deianira, approaches and
> detains her while the others pass indoors.*)

Messenger

Wait! Stay a moment here that you may learn,   335
without these others, who they are that you lead inside,
and, since you have heard nothing at all, you may discover
what you must. For of all this I have knowledge.

Deianira

What do you want? Why have you stopped me from going in?

Messenger

Stay and hear me. The earlier message you had from me   340
was no waste of time, nor, I think, will this be.

Deianira

Should we call the others back, or do you wish
to speak only to me and to my friends here?

Messenger

    To you and your friends I may speak—leave the others.

Deianira

    They are gone now, so please give me an explanation.   345

Messenger

    Nothing that man has just been telling you was spoken
    in strict honesty. Either he is a liar now,
    or he was no honest messenger before.

Deianira

    What are you saying? Tell me clearly everything
    you know. I cannot understand what you have said.   350

Messenger

    I myself heard this man say—and many men
    were present who can bear me out—that for the sake
    of this girl Heracles destroyed Eurytus
    and his high-towered Oechalia; and, of the Gods, it was
    Love alone who bewitched him into this violence—   355
    not his laborious service in Lydia for Omphale,
    nor the fact that Iphitus was hurled to his death—
    it was Love, whom he brushes aside in this new version.
    But the truth is that when he could not persuade the father
    to give the child to him for his secret bed,   360
    he fabricated a petty complaint, an excuse
    to campaign against the girl's country, and sacked   362/364
    the city. And now, as you see, he is coming home   365
    and has sent her here, not without a reason, lady,
    and not to be a slave. You must not expect that!
    It would not be likely if he is inflamed with desire.
    So I thought it best to reveal the whole affair
    to you, my mistress, just as I happened to hear it from him,   370
    and there were many others listening to this same story
    in the public gathering of the men of Trachis who can
    refute him as well as I. If what I say is unkind,
    I am sorry, but still I have told the strict truth.

Deianira

Oh! Oh! What has happened to me? I have   375
welcomed a secret enemy under my roof.
Oh, I am miserable, miserable! How truly nameless
is she, as the man who brought her swore to me—
a girl so brilliant in her looks and in her birth!

Messenger

Yes, she had Eurytus for her father and was called   380
Iole, but of course *he* could tell you nothing
of her origin since he had never asked!

Chorus

Damn all scoundrels, but damn him most of all
who practices a secret, degrading villainy.

Deianira

What shall I do? I must ask you, for the story   385
which has now come out leaves me utterly stunned.

Chorus

Go and talk to Lichas. Perhaps he would speak out
if you insisted on knowing, whether he liked it or not.

Deianira

I shall go. Your advice is not unreasonable.

Messenger

Shall I wait meanwhile? What do you wish me to do?   390

Deianira

Stay, for I see the man has started from the house
of his own accord, without my summoning him.

(*Lichas enters from the house.*)

Lichas

Lady, what should I say when I come to Heracles?
Give me instructions, for, as you see, I am on my way.

Deianira

How quickly you are rushing off when you were   395
so long in coming, before we have even talked again.

Lichas

If there is anything you wish to ask me, I am at your service.

Deianira

Will I be able to trust in the truth of what you say?

Lichas

Yes—great Zeus be my witness!—as far as my knowledge goes.

Deianira

Tell me, then, who is the woman you brought with you?   400

Lichas

A Euboean. But I do not know her parents.

Messenger

You there! Look here! To whom do you think you are talking?

Lichas

And you—what do you mean asking such a question?

Messenger

You would be well advised to try to answer me.

Lichas

I speak to her who commands, Deianira, daughter   405
of Oeneus and the consort of Heracles, if my eyes
do not deceive me—it is my *mistress* that I address.

Messenger

There it is, the very thing I wanted to hear.
You say she is your mistress?

Lichas

It is the honest truth.

Messenger

Well, then, what do you think should be your punishment   410
if you are discovered to have been dishonest with her?

Lichas

What do you mean "dishonest"? What are these tricky riddles?

Messenger

No riddles at all! You are the one who is being tricky.

Lichas

I am leaving. I have been a fool to listen so long.

Messenger

Not yet, not before you answer a few questions.   415

Lichas

Say what you want. You'll not be at a loss for words.

Messenger

That captive girl whom you brought to the house, you know
whom I mean?

Lichas

              I do, but why do you ask about her?

Messenger

You look at her with no sign of recognition,
but did you not say she was Iole, the daughter of Eurytus?   420

Lichas

Where on earth did I say so? Who is going to come
and testify that he was there and heard me talk?

Messenger

You spoke before many of the townspeople. A large crowd
in the public place of Trachis heard you say this.

Lichas

Oh, yes—
They may have said they heard me. But to repeat an impression   425
is not the same as giving an accurate account.

Messenger

Impression, indeed! Did you not state under oath that you
were bringing this girl as a consort for Heracles?

Lichas

I said that? By the Gods, explain to me,
dear mistress—this stranger here, who on earth is he?   430

Messenger

A man who was there and heard you say her city was

completely crushed through desire for her; no woman
of Lydia destroyed it, but his clear love for her.

Lichas

Please have this fellow leave. No sensible person,
mistress, wastes his time exchanging words with a madman.   435

Deianira

By Zeus who flashes lightning over the topmost glen
of Oeta, do not cheat me of the truth! Speak,
and you will find that I am not a spiteful woman
nor one who does not know how it is with man—
we cannot always enjoy a constant happiness.   440
How foolish one would be to climb into the ring
with Love and try to trade blows with him, like a boxer.
For he rules even the Gods as he pleases, and
he rules me—why not another woman like me?
You see that I would be altogether mad   445
to blame my husband, because he suffers from this sickness,
or that woman. She has been guilty of nothing shameful,
and she has done no harm to me. No, it is
inconceivable. If you have learned to lie from him,
then you are not learning honest lessons. If you school   450
yourself in this fashion, you succeed only
in seeming dishonest when you are trying to be decent.
Tell me the whole truth. To gain the reputation
of a liar is utter dishonor for a free man.
You cannot think that I will not hear. There are   455
many men to whom you have spoken, and they will tell me.

                    (Deianira pauses, but Lichas remains silent.)
Are you afraid of hurting me? You are wrong.
The only thing that could hurt would be not to know.
Where is the danger in knowing? One man and many women—
Heracles has had other women before.   460
Never yet has one of them earned insults
from me, or spiteful talk, nor will *she*, even
if she is utterly absorbed in her passion,

for I pitied her deeply when I saw her because
her own beauty has destroyed her life, and, against her will,　465
this unfortunate girl has sacked and enslaved the land
of her fathers. Now let all this flow away
on the wind. To you I have this to say: You may
be dishonest with others, but never lie to me.

Chorus

Obey her. What she says is good. You will have　470
no cause to complain later, and you will gain our thanks.

Lichas

Well, dear mistress, I realize that you are not
unreasonable. You see things as we mortals must.
So I shall tell you the whole truth. I shall not hide it.
It is just as this man said. A terrible longing　475
ran through Heracles—and it *was* for this girl.
Because of her, Oechalia, the land of her fathers,
was overthrown by his spear with great destruction.
None of this did he tell me to hide, I must say
in fairness to him; none of this did he ever deny.　480
I myself, O my mistress, was fearful lest I
should cause pain in your breast by these words of mine.
It was I who erred, if you would call this error.
But since, as it turns out, you know the whole story,
for your own sake as much as for his, be kind　485
to the woman and show that the words you spoke to her
before you knew were said in all sincerity.
Against all else he has won by sheer strength; but by
this love for her he has been completely vanquished.

Deianira

Those are my feelings too, and so too shall I act.　490
You may be sure I shall not choose to add to my
afflictions hopeless resistance to the Gods. Now let us
go into the house. I have messages for you
to carry, and there are gifts to match the gifts you brought—
these too you must take. It would not be right to leave　495
empty-handed when you came so well provided.

(Deianira and Lichas and perhaps the Messenger,
who must be rewarded, enter the house.)

Chorus

Strong is the victory the Cyprian Goddess always wins.
I pass by
the Gods; I would not tell how Zeus was tricked by her;   500
nor Hades, who lives in the night;
nor Poseidon, the shaker of the earth.
But for our lady's hand
who were the two valiant contenders in courtship?
Who were they who came out to struggle in bouts that were   505
all blows and all dust?

One was a strong river with the looks of a high-horned
four-footed bull,
Acheloüs from Oeniadae; the other   510
came from the Thebes of Bacchus,
shaking his back-sprung bow, his spears and club
—the son of Zeus. They came
together then in the middle, desiring
her bed. Alone, in the middle with them, their referee,   515
Cypris, goddess of love's bed.

Then there was thudding of fists and clang of bows
and confusion of bulls' horns;
and there was contorted grappling,   520
and there were deadly blows from butting heads
and groaning on both sides.
But the tender girl with the lovely
eyes sat far from them on a hillside,
waiting for the one who would be her husband.   525
So the struggle raged, as I have told it;
but the bride over whom they fought
awaited the end pitiably.
And then she was gone from her mother,
like a calf that is lost.   530

(Deianira comes out from the house.)

Deianira

    Dear friends, while our visitor is in the house
talking to the captured girls before he leaves,
I have come out to you, unobserved. I want
to tell you the work my hands have done, but also to have
your sympathy as I cry out for all I suffer.   535
For here I have taken on a girl—no,
I can think that no longer—a married woman, as
a ship's master takes on cargo, goods that outrage my heart.
So now the two of us lie under the one sheet
waiting for his embrace. This is the gift my brave   540
and faithful Heracles sends home to his dear wife
to compensate for his long absence! And yet, when he
is sick as he so often is with this same sickness,
I am incapable of anger. But to live
in the same house with her, to share the same marriage,   545
that is something else. What woman could stand that?
For I see her youth is coming to full bloom
while mine is fading. The eyes of men love to pluck
the blossoms; from the faded flowers they turn away.
And this is why I am afraid that he may   550
be called my husband but be the younger woman's man.
But no sensible woman, as I've said before,
should let herself give way to rage. I shall tell you,
dear friends, the solution I have to bring myself relief.

    I have had hidden in a copper urn   555
for many years the gift of a centaur, long ago.
While I was still a child, I took it from the wounds
of the hairy-chested Nessus as he was dying.
He used to ferry people, for a fee, across
the deep flood of the Evenus, in his arms   560
with no oars to drive him over nor ships' sails.
I too was carried on his shoulders when my father
sent me to follow Heracles for the first time

as his wife. When I was halfway across
his hands touched me lustfully. I cried out and at once   565
the son of Zeus turned around, raised his hands,
and shot a feathered arrow through his chest; into
his lungs it hissed. The beast spoke his last words to me
as he died: "Daughter of old Oeneus,
if you listen to me, you shall have great profit   570
from my ferrying, since you are the last I have brought across.
If you take in your hands this blood, clotted in
my wounds, wherever it is black with the bile
of the Hydra, the monstrous serpent of Lerna, in which
he dipped his arrows, you will have a charm over   575
the heart of Heracles, so he will never look
at another woman and love her more than you."
I have thought of this, my friends, for since his death
I have kept it in the house, tightly closed.
I followed all instructions he gave me while he still lived   580
and dipped this robe in the charm. Now it is all done.

I am not a woman who tries to be—and may
I never learn to be—bad and bold. I hate
women who are. But if somehow by these charms,
these spells I lay on Heracles, I can defeat   585
the girl—well, the move is made, unless you think
I am acting rashly. If so, I shall stop.

Chorus
    If there is reason for confidence in these measures,
    you do not seem to us to have acted badly.

Deianira
    I have this much confidence only: there seem to be   590
    good prospects, but I have never brought them to the test.

Chorus
    One can only tell from action. Whatever you think,
    you have no way of judging before you try it out.

Deianira

    Well, we shall know soon. I see the messenger
    coming out of doors, and he will be going shortly.   595
    Only be discreet. In darkness one may be
    ashamed of what one does, without the shame of disgrace.

                    (Lichas comes out from the house.)

Lichas

    What would you wish me to do? Command me, O daughter of
      Oeneus.
    I have already stayed too long, and now I am late.

Deianira

    Lichas, this is the very thing I have looked after   600
    while you were talking to the foreign women inside.
    Here is a gift made by my own hands for you
    to take to my husband—this long, fine-woven robe.
    When you give it to him, you must tell him that it
    should touch the skin of no man before it touches his,   605
    nor should he let the light of the sun look upon it,
    nor any holy inclosure, nor the gleam from a hearth,
    until he himself stands, conspicuous before all,
    and shows it to the Gods on a day of bull-slaughtering.
    For this was my vow: if I should ever see or hear   610
    that he was coming safe to his home, in all piety
    I would dress him in this robe to appear before
    the Gods to make new sacrifice in new clothing.
    And you shall carry a token of this vow which he
    will understand from the familiar encircled print   615
    of my seal.
            Go now, and as a messenger
    be sure to keep the rule not to exceed your orders.
    In this way, with thanks both from my husband and
    from me, you will earn our double gratitude.

Lichas

    If I, the messenger, practice this art of Hermes   620
    soundly, I shall never fail in serving you.

I shall present this chest exactly as it is,
and in explanation I shall repeat your words.

Deianira

Then you should be going now. You understand
completely how everything is here in this house.   625

Lichas

I understand, and I shall report that all is well.

Deianira

And, of course, since you saw it, you know the girl's
reception—you know I received her as a friend.

Lichas

Yes, I do, and I am astonished and delighted.

Deianira

What else is there to tell him? For I am afraid   630
you would be talking too soon of my longing for him
before I know if *he* feels longing for me.

  (*Exit Lichas through a side entrance; Deianira enters the house.*)

Chorus

Safe harbors, hot-springs among
the rocks, the high cliffs of Oeta—
all you who live by these and by the inmost reaches   635
of the sea in Malis,
the coast of the Maid who shoots the golden shaft,
and there at the Gates,
the famous gatherings of the Greeks—

Soon again the lovely cries   640
of the flute will rise among you;
now it will not ring in disagreeable clamor
but like the lyre, music
for the gods. The son of Zeus and Alcmena
hurries to his home   645
bearing the prizes of all valor.

Gone from the city completely,
we missed him, waiting a long twelve months, while he
was on the sea, but we knew
nothing, and his loving wife   650
all lamentation always, sadly, most
sadly, broke her heart.
But now Ares, God of War,
stung to madness, dispels her day of troubles.

Oh let him come, let him come,   655
and his ship of many oars; let it
not stop before he ends his journey
at this city, leaving the island
hearth where, they say, he makes sacrifice.
Let him come from there   660
all desire when the beast's
inducements, all dipped in persuasion, have melted him.

                    (*Deianira comes out from the house.*)

Deianira

O my friends, I am afraid! Can it be
I have gone too far in all I have just done?

Chorus

What is the matter, Deianira, child of Oeneus?   665

Deianira

I don't know. I have a foreboding that I'll be shown
to have done great harm when I hoped to do good.

Chorus

Surely you do not mean your gift to Heracles?

Deianira

Yes, yes. Now I see that one should never
plunge eagerly into anything obscure.   670

Chorus

Explain the cause of your fear, if it can be explained.

Deianira

    Something has happened which, if I tell you, my friends,
    will seem a marvel such as you never thought to hear.
    Just now, when I anointed the robe I sent to be
    my husband's vestment, I used a tuft of fleecy white wool.   675
    This piece has disappeared, devoured by nothing in
    the house but destroyed by itself, eaten away
    and crumbled completely to dust. I want to tell you this
    in detail, so you may know the whole story.

    I neglected none of the instructions that beast   680
    the centaur explained to me, lying in agony
    with the sharp arrowhead in his side. I kept them
    like an inscription on bronze that cannot be washed away.
    And I only did what I was told to do—
    I must keep this drug away from fire and always   685
    deep in the house where no warm ray of light may touch it
    until I should want to apply it freshly smeared.
    And this is what I did. Now, when it had to do its work,
    at home, inside the house, secretly I smeared it on
    some wool, a scrap I pulled from one of the household sheep,   690
    and then I folded my gift and put it in a chest
    before the sun could shine on it, as you saw.

    But when I go in again, I see something
    unspeakable, incomprehensible to human reason.
    Somehow I had happened to throw the ball of wool,   695
    which I had used to smear the robe, into the full heat
    of the sun's rays, and, as it became warm,
    it all ran together, a confused mass, and crumbled
    to bits on the ground, looking most like the dust one sees
    eaten away in the cutting of a piece of wood.   700
    Like this it lies where it fell. But from the earth
    on which it rests, clotted foam boils up
    like the rich liquid of the blue-green fruit
    from the vines of Dionysus, poured on the earth.

And now I do not know what to think. I see   705
myself as someone who has done a terrible thing.
From what possible motive, in return for what,
could the dying beast have shown me kindness, when he
was dying because of me? No, he beguiled me,
only to destroy the man who shot him. But I   710
have come to understand now when it is too late.
I alone, unless my fears are fanciful,
I, his unhappy wife, shall destroy him.
I know that arrow which struck Nessus injured even
Chiron, who was a god, and all animals,   715
whatever it touches, it kills. This same poison which seeped,
black and bloody, from the wounds of Nessus, how can
it fail to kill Heracles too? At least, this is
my fear. And yet I have made a decision: if he goes down,
under the same blow I will die with him.   720
I could not bear to live and hear myself called evil
when my only wish is to be truly good.

Chorus
Terrible results are appalling, but one
should not expect the worst before anything has happened.

Deianira
When the plans themselves are bad, there can be   725
no expectations that leave any place for courage.

Chorus
But whenever we trip up unwillingly,
the anger felt is tempered, and so it should be with you.

Deianira
You may talk like this, since you have no share
in the wrong; you have no burden all your own.   730

Chorus
Better to be silent now—say nothing more,
if you do not want to tell it to your son.
The one who went away to search for his father is here.

(Hyllus enters from the side.)

Hyllus

    Mother! I wish I could have found you not as you are
    but no longer alive, or safe but someone else's   735
    mother, or somehow changed and with a better heart
    than now. Three ways—Oh, for any one of them!

Deianira

    My son, what has happened that I should be so hateful?

Hyllus

    What has happened? Your husband, my father—
    do you hear me?—you have killed him.   740

Deianira

    No, no, my child! What have you blurted out?

Hyllus

    Only what cannot fail to be. Once a thing
    is seen, who can cause it never to have been?

Deianira

    How could you say it? Who on earth told you
    that I did this awful crime you charge me with?   745

Hyllus

    I saw my father's heavy fall with my own eyes
    myself; I did not hear of it from anyone.

Deianira

    Where did you come upon him? Were you at his side?

Hyllus

    If you must hear, then I must talk and tell you all.
    When he sacked the famous city of Eurytus,   750
    he marched away with the trophies and the first-fruits of victory.
    On a wave-beaten shore of Euboea there is
    a point called Cenaeum, where he marked out altars
    and a whole precinct for Zeus, god of our fathers.
    There I first saw him, glad after my longing.   755
    He was about to make great slaughter for sacrifice

when his own herald Lichas arrived from our home,
bringing with him that gift of yours, the deadly robe.
He clothed himself in it just as you had instructed
and killed first his bulls, twelve perfect victims,   760
the pick of the booty; then he brought the number to
one hundred, driving a mixed herd to the altar.
And at first the poor wretch, his mind at ease,
rejoicing in his handsome dress, prayed to the Gods.
But as the flame from the juicy pine-wood fire   765
blazed high and bloody from the solemn rites,
the sweat broke out on his skin; the robe enfolded him
around his limbs, joined tightly to his sides
like the work of a sculptor. Spasms of pain
bit into his bones. Then like the vicious, murderous   770
viper's poison, it began to consume him.

Now he shouted for that unfortunate Lichas, who was
in no way guilty of your crime, demanding
to know the plot behind his bringing him this robe.
Unlucky man, he knew nothing and said it was   775
a gift from you alone, just as you had sent it.
And at that moment, as Heracles listened to his answer,
a piercing, tearing pain clutched at his lungs; he caught
Lichas by the foot where the ankle turns
and threw him against a wave-beaten rock that juts from the sea.   780
It pressed the pale brains out through his hair,
and, split full on, skull and blood mixed and spread.
All the people there cried out in horror for
the one man in his suffering, the other dead.
No one had the courage to come to Heracles.   785
He would be wrenched now to the ground, now in the air,
crying, shrieking. All around the rocks echoed,
the mountain headlands of Locris, the high cliffs of Euboea.
When he gave up at last, after throwing himself
miserably again and again to the earth, crying   790

and groaning again and again, damning the mismating
in your wretched bed, the whole marriage that he
had won from Oeneus, only to befoul his life,
he raised his eyes, distorted, from the dark smoke
that hung around him and saw me in the great crowd,   795
tears pouring down my face, and, looking at me, called:
"My son, come to me! Do not run from me
in my pain, even if you must die with me.
Take me away! Above all else I ask you to put me
in a place where no man can look at me.   800
If you have pity, at least carry me out of this land
as soon as you can, that I may not die here."
These were his orders; we placed him in the middle of
a boat and with difficulty landed him here,
howling in spasms of pain. You shall be seeing him   805
at once, still alive or dead only now.

Mother, this is what you have planned and done to my father,
and you are caught. For this, Justice who punishes
and the Fury will requite you. If it is right
for a son, I curse you, and it *is* right, since you   810
have given me the right by killing the best of all men
on earth, such as you shall never see again.

(*Deianira moves away and leaves by the side.*)

Chorus (*to Deianira*)

Why do you go off in silence? Surely you see
that by silence you join your accuser and accuse yourself?

Hyllus

Let her go, and I hope a fair wind blows   815
to carry her far out of my sight. For why should she
maintain the pointless dignity of the name
of mother when she acts in no way like a mother?
No, let her go—goodbye to her. And the delight
she gave my father, may she find the same herself.   820

(*Hyllus enters the house.*)

Chorus

    See, maidens, how, suddenly, it has closed
    with us, the prophetic word spoken
    with foreknowledge long ago, that said
    when the year of the twelfth plowing came to an end,
    then it would bring an end for the true-born son of Zeus   825
    to his relay of toils. And now, surely,
    at the right time, it all comes home.
    How can he who no longer sees
    still have, still, toilsome
    servitude, when he is dead?   830

    If there clings to him in a murderous cloud
    the centaur's treacherous, sure trap
    and his sides are soaked with venom
    that Death begat and the shimmering serpent bred,
    how shall he see another sun after today's   835
    when the Hydra, horrible and monstrous, has
    soaked in? From the black-maned beast's
    treacherous words there comes to torture him
    a murderous confusion,
    sharp points brought to burning heat.   840

    She, poor woman, knew nothing of this
    but, seeing great injury for her home
    from a new marriage swiftly approaching,
    applied her remedy;   845
    but what came from another's will, a fatal meeting,
    truly, lost, she laments,
    truly, she weeps a pale,
    foaming flood of tears. Doom
    as it advances makes clear before
    it comes a great disaster from treachery.   850

    A spring of tears burst open.
    Such sickness, alas, has poured upon him, suffering
    to pity as never yet came upon the hero

from his enemies.   855
Woe for the dark head of the front-fighting spear
that won in battle this
fatal bride from steep
Oechalia. But that silent
handmaiden, Cyprian Aphrodite,   860
is revealed; it is her work.

                    (*Wailing is heard inside the house.*)

Chorus (*the women speak separately throughout this scene*)
    Can I be mistaken? Do I hear something,
    a cry of grief surging now through the house?

    What can I say?   865
    The sound is all too clear. They are shrieking for
    misfortune inside. The house suffers a new blow.

                    (*The Nurse comes out of the house.*)

    And see
    this old woman who is coming toward us, to tell us
    something, see how sad she is and how she frowns.   870

Nurse
    O maidens, that gift she sent to Heracles,
    truly it was the beginning of great sorrow for us.

Chorus
    What new calamity have you to tell us, old woman?

Nurse
    Deianira, motionless, has moved away
    to start upon the very last of all her journeys.   875

Chorus
    No, you cannot mean she is dead?

Nurse
                                    You know all.

Chorus
    Then she is dead, the poor woman?

Nurse
                                    I tell you again, she is.

Chorus

Gone, poor thing! Can you tell us how she died?

Nurse

Horrible, the way it happened!

Chorus

                    Tell us, woman,

the fate she met   880

Nurse

She destroyed herself.

Chorus

Was her mind in a passion or sick?

Nurse

The weapon's cruel point
killed her.

Chorus

            How could she think of
death on top of death   885
and end her life all alone?

Nurse

The grim steel cut her.

Chorus

And helpless did you see her awful act?

Nurse

Yes, I saw it. For I was standing near her there.

Chorus

Oh, what was it? How? Tell us.   890

Nurse

She herself by herself set her hand to it.

Chorus

What are you saying?

Nurse

            The clear truth.

Chorus

    That bride, newly come,
    has borne, has borne a mighty
    Fury for this house.   895

Nurse

    Yes, and if you had been near and had seen
    what Deianira did, still more would you pity.

Chorus

    How could any woman bring her hands to this?

Nurse

    Yes, it was terrible. You will learn everything
    and bear me witness. When she went into the house, alone,   900
    and saw her son in the courtyard, arranging a cushioned bed
    to take with him as he went back to meet his father,
    she hid herself where no one might look at her and groaned,
    falling against the altars, that now they would be
    deserted; and whenever she touched some household thing   905
    she used to use before, the poor creature would weep.
    Here and there, from room to room, she kept turning,
    and if she saw some servant of the household who was
    dear to her, she would look at her sadly and weep,
    and she would call out loud to her fate and to   910
    her house that would have no children any more.

    Then she stops all this, and suddenly I see her
    rushing into the bedchamber of Heracles,
    and secretly, from the shadows, I keep watch
    over her. I see the woman casting sheets   915
    and spreading them upon the bed of Heracles.
    Then, as soon as she had finished, she leapt up
    and sat there in the middle of her marriage bed,
    and, bursting into torrents of hot tears, she said:
    "O my bed, O my bridal chamber, farewell   920
    now forever, for never again will you take me
    to lie as a wife between these sheets of yours."

She says nothing more, but with a violent sweep
of her arm unfastens her gown where a pin
of beaten gold lies above her breast. She had   925
uncovered her whole side and her left arm.
And I go running off with all the strength I have
and tell her son what his mother is planning to do.
But in the time I have been rushing there and back
we see that she has cut her side to the liver   930
and the seat of life with a double-bladed sword.
Her son shrieked, for he realized, poor boy,
that in his anger he had forced her to this act.
He had just learned from people in the house that she
had done unwittingly the will of the beast.   935

Then the miserable boy abandoned himself utterly
to sobs and mourning for his mother; he threw himself
upon her lips and there, pressing his side to hers,
he lay and groaned over and over that he
had struck her thoughtlessly with a cruel accusation,   940
weeping because at one moment he was doubly
orphaned for all his life, losing his father and her.

> (*The Nurse throws open the doors of the house, revealing*
> *Hyllus and the body of Deianira,*
> *lying on a couch.*)

This is the way things are within. If anyone
counts upon one day ahead or even more,
he does not think. For there can be no tomorrow   945
until we have safely passed the day that is with us still.

> (*The Nurse enters the house.*)

Chorus
   Which shall I lament first?
   Which is the more final disaster?
   In my distress I cannot tell.
   The one we can see in the house,   950

the other besets us in our thoughts—
to have and to await are the same.

Oh for a strong blast
of fair wind coming to my hearth
to carry me away from this place   955
that I may not die of fright
when I no more than look
at Zeus's valiant son.
They say he is coming to the house
in unassuageable pain,   960
a wonder beyond telling.

(*Men enter from the side, carrying Heracles in a litter,
accompanied by an old man; Hyllus enters from
the house, closing the doors after him.*)

Near, then, not distant
is he for whom I cried, like the shrill
nightingale. Here strangers are approaching.   965
How are they carrying him? As though
mourning for a friend,
their steps are slow, soundless.
Ah! He is carried without a word.
Am I to think that he
is dead or only asleep?   970

Hyllus

O my father!
O my sorrow! What is left
for me? How can I help?

Old Man

Be silent, child, do not excite
the wild pain that makes him savage.   975
He still lives, though fallen. You must
bite your lips.

Hyllus

      What? Alive?

Old Man

    Do not wake him, held fast in sleep.
    Do not excite, do not set stirring
    that awful returning
    sickness.   980

Hyllus

           But it drives me mad,
    so helpless under an immense weight!

Heracles

    O Zeus,
    what land have I come to? Among what men
    do I lie worn out by these   985
    unceasing pains? O my agony!
    The filthy thing eats me again.

Old Man

    Now do you see how much better it was
    to hide your sorrow in silence, nor shatter
    sleep from his head   990
    and eyes?

Hyllus

           No, I cannot stand it
    when I see him in this suffering.

Heracles

    O altar steps of Cenaeum, is this
    all the thanks you win me for all
    the sacrifice I made on you?
    O Zeus! Torture, torture is all   995
    you give me! I wish I had never seen you
    with these poor eyes that must face now
    this inexorable flowering of madness.
    Is there any singer of spells,   1000
    any craftsman surgeon who can
    exorcise this curse, but Zeus?
    Even to see him would be a wonder!

(*The bearers set the litter down.*)

Oh! Let me be. Let
me sleep in my misery,   1005
let me sleep my last sleep.

Where are you touching me? Where are you laying me?
You are killing me, killing me.
You have prodded awake what slumbered.

It has caught me. Oh! It comes on again.   1010
O most ungrateful of the Greeks, where are all you
for whom I destroyed myself purging so many beasts
from all the seas and woods? Now when *I* am sick,
will no one turn the beneficial fire, the sword on me?

Oh! Why will no one   1015
come and cut away
my head from my abominable body.

(*The Old Man tries to restrain and support Heracles.*)

Old Man

    Come, you are the man's son. The task is more
than my strength can manage. You must help. Your strength
can easily do more for him than I.

Hyllus

                  I touch him,   1020
but to make him unconscious of pain, that is beyond
my power or any man's. Such is the will of Zeus.

Heracles

    My son, my son! where are you? Help me, here,
here, lift me up. Oh! Oh! My fate!   1025

It lunges, lunges again, the vile thing
is destroying me—
savage, unapproachable sickness.   1030

O Pallas! It is torturing me again. O my son,
pity me who begot you, draw the sword—no one   1035

will blame you—strike me in the breast, heal the pain
with which your godless mother has made me rage. Oh
to see her fallen, felled by this death she deals me!   1040

Sweet Hades, kinsman, brother of Zeus, lull me to sleep,
to sleep; with quick death end my agony.

Chorus

My friends, I hear and shudder at the king's misfortunes—
so great a man, hounded by such suffering.   1045

Heracles

Many are the toils for these hands, this back,
that I have had, hot and painful even to tell of.
But neither the wife of Zeus nor hateful Eurystheus
has ever condemned me to such agony as this
that the false-faced daughter of Oeneus has fastened   1050
upon my shoulders, a woven, encircling net
of the Furies, by which I am utterly destroyed.
It clings to my sides, it has eaten away
my inmost flesh; it lives with me and empties the channels
of my lungs, and already it has drunk up   1055
my fresh blood, and my whole body is
completely killed, conquered by these unspeakable fetters.
Neither the spear of battle, nor the army of
the earth-born Giants, nor the violence of beasts,
nor Greece, nor any place of barbarous tongue, not all   1060
the lands I came to purify could ever do this.
A woman, a female, in no way like a man,
she alone without even a sword has brought me down.

O my son, now truly be my true-born son
and do not pay more respect to the name of mother.   1065
Bring her from the house with your own hands and put
her in my hands, that woman who bore you, that I may know
clearly whether it pains you more to see *my* body
mutilated or *hers* when it is justly tortured.
Come, my child, dare to do this. Pity me,   1070

for I seem pitiful to many others, crying
and sobbing like a girl, and no one could ever say
that he had seen this man act like that before.
Always without a groan I followed my painful course.
Now in my misery I am discovered a woman.   1075

Come close to me now, stand by your father and
look well at my misfortune, see what I suffer.
I shall take off the coverings and show you. Look,
all of you, do you behold this poor body?
Can you see how miserable, how pitiful I am?   1080

Oh, oh, the pain!
That malignant tearing scorches me again,
it shoots through my sides, it *will* have me struggle,
it will not let me be—miserable, devouring sickness.
O King Hades, receive me!   1085
O flash of Zeus, strike!
Drive against me, O King, hurl down the bolt
of lightning, Father. Now it feeds on me again,
it has sprung out, it blooms. O my hands, my hands,
O my back, my chest, O my poor arms, see   1090
what has become of you from what you once were.
The lion that prowled the land of Nemea, that scourge of herds-
    men,
that unapproachable, intractable creature,
with your strength once you overpowered it,
and the serpent of Lerna and that galloping army   1095
of double-bodied, hostile beasts, violent, lawless,
supremely strong, and the boar of Erymanthus,
and under the earth the hell hound with three heads,
irresistible monster, the awful Echidna's whelp,
and guarding the golden apples the dragon at the end of the
    earth—   1100
and I have had my taste of ten thousand other toils,
but these hands let no one set his trophies over me.

Now look at me, torn to shreds, my limbs unhinged,
a miserable ruin sacked by invisible disaster, I
who am called the son of the most noble mother,   1105
I who claim to be begotten of Zeus in the heavens.
But I tell you this, even if I am nothing,
nothing that can even crawl, even so—
only let her come who has done this to me—
these hands will teach her, and she can tell the world: alive   1110
I punished the evil, and I punish them in death.

Chorus

O unhappy Greece, I can see how great
a mourning you shall have if you lose this man.

Hyllus

Father, since you let me speak to you now,
let me have silence while I speak, though you are sick.   1115
I ask only for what is right. Give me yourself
without this grim anger which stings you to such fury.
Otherwise you cannot know how mistaken
is the pleasure your fury craves, the pain it feels.

Heracles

Say what you want and be done with it. I am too sick—   1120
I can make no sense at all of your riddles.

Hyllus

It is about my mother that I come to speak,
about her present state and her unwilling error.

Heracles

Damn you! How dare you speak of her again, the mother
Who is a father's murderer—and in my hearing?   1125

Hyllus

Her state is such that one should not keep silent.

Heracles

No, no silence for the crime she has committed!

Hyllus

Nor for what she has done today, you will admit.

Heracles

Speak, but beware. Do not disgrace yourself.

Hyllus

I shall speak. She is dead. She has just been killed.   1130

Heracles

By whom? I cannot believe it. It is too bitter news.

Hyllus

She is dead by her own hand and by no other.

Heracles

Ah! She's dead too soon. She should have died by mine.

Hyllus

Even your fury would turn aside if you knew all.

Heracles

A strange beginning, but go on—what do you mean?   1135

Hyllus

In all that she did wrong she had intended good.

Heracles

Good? Does she do good when she kills your father?

Hyllus

It was a charm for love she wanted to put on you
that failed—when she saw that marriage in her house.

Heracles

Who in Trachis knows such deadly drugs as this?   1140

Hyllus

Nessus the centaur long ago persuaded her
to excite your desire with this fatal charm.

Heracles

Woe, woe is me! This is my miserable end.
Lost! I am lost! I see the light no longer.
Ah! Now I know the doom that is upon me.   1145
Come, my child. You no longer have a father.
Call together all my children, your brothers,

and call the unhappy Alcmena who was the bride of Zeus
to her cost. You shall learn from me with my
last words all the prophecies I know.   1150

Hyllus

But your mother is not here. It happens that
she is living now at Tiryns on the sea,
and of your children she has taken some with her
to care for, and others, I must tell you, are living in Thebes.
But all of us who are here—if there is anything,   1155
Father, we must do, we shall listen and serve you.

Heracles

Then hear your task. You have come to that point
where you must show the sort of man you are that you
are called my son. Long ago my father revealed
to me that I should die by nothing that draws breath   1160
but by someone dead, an inhabitant of Hell.
This was that beast, the centaur, who has in death killed me
alive, even as it had been divinely revealed.
Now I shall show you how more recent prophecies
agree with this exactly and give support to the old.   1165
I went to the grove of the mountain-dwelling Selli who sleep
upon the ground and I copied down the words
from my father's oak that speaks with many tongues,
which told me that, at this present, living time,
release from all the toils imposed on me would be   1170
complete. And I thought that then I would be happy.
But it only meant that I would die then.
For the dead there are no more toils. My son,
since all this is coming true so clearly, you must
be ready to stand by my side in the fight, and you must not   1175
hesitate till I am forced to use sharp words.
On your own, agree to act with me; discover
yourself the finest rule—obedience to your father.

Hyllus

Father, I am alarmed to see where your words lead,
but I shall obey you in whatever you decide.   1180

Heracles

You must give me your right hand first of all.

Hyllus

Will you tell me why you must have this strong pledge?

Heracles

Quickly, give me your hand. Do not disobey me.

Hyllus

Here, I reach my hand. I shall deny you nothing.

Heracles

Swear now by the head of Zeus who begot me.   1185

Hyllus

Swear to do what? Will you tell me that?

Heracles

Swear to fulfil completely the task I give to you.

Hyllus

I do swear, and I take my oath on Zeus.

Heracles

And pray for punishment if you break your oath.

Hyllus

I pray, though I shall keep my oath and not be punished.   1190

Heracles

You know that high crag of Zeus on Mount Oeta?

Hyllus

Yes. I have often stood there to sacrifice.

Heracles

Then you must take my body up there, with your
own hands and with the help of any friends you wish,
and you must fell a great forest of deep-rooted oak,   1195
and many trees of the lusty wild olive

you must cut down as well, and put my body on them,
and then take the flaming brand of a pine torch
and burn. Let me have no tears, no mourning. Do
your job without lamentation, without tears,   1200
if you are your father's son, or even below
I shall wait for you, a crushing curse forever.

Hyllus

Oh! What are you saying? What have you forced me to do?

Heracles

What must be done. If you do not do it, then be
another man's son—do not call yourself mine.   1205

Hyllus

Father, Father, how can you? You are asking me
to be your murderer, polluted with your blood.

Heracles

No, I am not. I ask you to be my healer,
the only physician who can cure my suffering.

Hyllus

How would I cure your body by setting it on fire?   1210

Heracles

If that frightens you, do the rest at least.

Hyllus

I shall carry you there—that I could not begrudge you.

Heracles

And you will complete the pyre as I told you?

Hyllus

So long as I do not touch it with my own hands.
Everything else I shall do. You can be sure of me.   1215

Heracles

Even that much is enough. Now after your other
great kindness, do me this one small favor.

Hyllus

No matter how great a favor it is, it shall be done.

Heracles

You know, of course, the girl who is the daughter of Eurytus?

Hyllus

It is Iole you mean, I suppose.   1220

Heracles

I see you know her. This, then, is what I tell you to do,
my son. When I die, if you wish to be pious
and remember the oaths you have sworn to your father,
you must take this girl as your wife, and do not
disobey me. No other man but you must ever   1225
have her who has lain with me at my side. You,
my son, must engage yourself to her bed.
Obey. Although you listen to me in greater matters,
disobedience in lesser things wipes out the favor.

Hyllus

Ah! It is wrong to argue with a sick man,   1230
yet how can one stand to see him with such thoughts as these?

Heracles

You speak as if you would do none of the things I ask.

Hyllus

How could anyone when she alone shares
the blame for my mother's death and your condition?
How could anyone choose to do that, unless   1235
avenging fiends had made his mind sick? Better
for me, too, to die than live with my worst enemy.

Heracles

I see the man will not give me my due, though I
am dying; but I tell you, if you disobey
my commands, the curse of the Gods will be waiting for you.   1240

Hyllus

Oh! Soon, I can see, you will show how sick you are.

Heracles

You! You rouse my agony from its sleep.

Hyllus

So wretched, so helpless am I, no matter where I turn.

Heracles

Because you do not choose to listen to your father.

Hyllus

But shall I listen, Father, and learn impiety?   1245

Heracles

It is no impiety if you give my heart pleasure.

Hyllus

Do you command me and make it right for me to do this?

Heracles

I do command you, and I call the Gods to witness.

Hyllus

I shall do it then, and I shall not forswear
since you have shown the Gods it is your will. No one   1250
could think me wrong in obeying you, Father.

Heracles

In the end you act well. Now make your mercy
follow swift upon your words. Put me on
the pyre before another tearing, stinging blow
can strike. Come, hurry. Lift me up. The true   1255
respite from suffering is this—my final end.

Hyllus

Nothing can prevent its full accomplishment
for you, since you command and compel me, Father.

Heracles

Come then, O my tough soul,
before this sickness is stirred again,   1260
set a steel bit in my mouth,
hold back the shriek, and make an end
of this unwanted, welcome task.

(*The bearers raise the litter and leave by the side,
followed by Hyllus and the Chorus.*)

Hyllus

    Raise him, my helpers. From you let me have
    much compassion now for what I do.   1265
    You see how little compassion the Gods
    have shown in all that's happened; they
    who are called our fathers, who begot us,
    can look upon such suffering.
    No one can foresee what is to come.   1270
    What is here now is pitiful for us
    and shameful for the Gods;
    but of all men it is hardest for him
    who is the victim of this disaster.

                 (*Hyllus turns to the leader of the Chorus.*)
    Maiden, come from the house with us.   1275
    You have seen a terrible death
    and agonies, many and strange, and there is
    nothing here which is not Zeus.

                                (*Exeunt.*)

ELECTRA

Translated by David Grene

INTRODUCTION TO THE
ELECTRA

I⊤ IS often said by classical scholars that, of the three dramatic treatments of the Orestes legend which we possess in the Greek tragedies, that of Sophocles stands closest to the Homeric account. Homer introduces the story of Orestes several times in the *Odyssey* and always for its exemplary effect. The return of Orestes and the punishment of Aegisthus, and only incidentally Clytemnestra, is mentioned as a warning of what will happen to the suitors when Odysseus comes home. Homer shows no awareness of the brutality of the murder of the mother by her son or of any of the consequences, religious or sociological, which interest both Aeschylus and Euripides later. The whole is a saga of successful revenge. It is worth noticing, of course, that Homer introduces the incident as an *example* of what may happen when Odysseus comes home. He is not giving us his speculations on matricide. Still, even at that, it is perhaps curious that the revenge taken, including the killing of Clytemnestra, can be treated with such clarity of moral judgment in favor of the killers.

In outline Sophocles appears to handle the story as Homer does, as a revenge theme, with no divine or other sanctions invoked against the murderers. But it is difficult to believe that Sophocles' interpretation should be taken on so simple a level. Almost forty-five years before the Sophoclean play, Aeschylus had written the *Oresteia*, which treated the legend with exactly the questions in mind that Homer had omitted. The *Oresteia* was a great popular success. It is extremely unlikely that Sophocles later could have reverted to the older and simpler explanation of the story without submitting a new interpretation of his own. The latter is, in fact, what he did.

He certainly did write with the Homeric outline in mind. For instance, in Aeschylus the responsibility for goading Orestes to kill both Aegisthus and Clytemnestra is Apollo's, and consequently the purification, with all its attendant complications and conflict, belongs to Apollo. Sophocles minimized Apollo's role, mentioning him only a few times in the play as the author of indefinitely favorable oracles. The question of the purification or of Orestes' madness after the killing of his mother does not arise. But Sophocles has used the very flatness of the Homeric version to emphasize the unspoken questions which are in the mind of his fifth-century audience. If this is simply a story of murder and the settlement of a family feud, including the killing of a mother by her son, we are given a special Sophoclean portrait of the figures involved—mother, daughter, son, and Aegisthus, but especially Electra, the elder daughter.

For the play is rightly called after Electra. All the other people are included, principally, so that we should know more about her when we see her dealing with them—the savage, yet frightened, mother; the cautious and rather colorless Orestes; the timid, sensible, and unattractive sister; and the vulgar and bullying Aegisthus. Everyone acts as the foil of Electra. Everyone brings out another shade in the character previously missing. Electra makes no soliloquies to reveal herself as she does in Euripides. She is herself, in relation to others. She seems hardly to exist as a person except as a combination of reactions to others' deeds and words. Her father's death, her mother's enmity, her sister's passiveness, her brother's delay, Aegisthus' tyranny—these are her life. She says again and again that they are the causes for her being what she is.

Furthermore, Sophocles shows us Electra in reaction to happenings that in fact never took place. The disguised Paedagogus gives a vivid account of a chariot race in which Orestes is killed, the whole story being false. Orestes arrives, disguised, accompanied by the urn which supposedly contains his own ashes. Both of these are remarkable incidents as we have them in the play. The chariot race which occupies nearly 200 lines, or almost one-seventh of the entire piece, is based partly on that described in the *Iliad*, Book xxiii. It may also be based partly on some famous contemporary chariot race in which the audience would be interested and of which we know nothing. But the more exciting the account, the more it engaged the audience's attention, the greater, surely, must have been the jolt when it was realized that the description corresponded to no dramatic reality.

The terrible grief felt by Electra when she saw the urn believed to contain her brother's ashes must have awakened a jarring emotion in the audience, who knew that he was not dead, and some resentment at Orestes for standing by his sister and not telling her. These things are too gross to be explained away by any contrast between the Athenian audience's expectation and those of the theater of our own time. I think we are meant to see Electra not as a real person in her own right but as a mass of responses to other persons and their deeds and words, whether true or false. It is hard to imagine her loving someone understandingly, as Tecmessa and Deianeira did. Husband-less, childless, as she describes herself, cut off from father and mother and sister, she moves in an atmosphere of hate and hysteria provoked by facts and lies indiscriminately.

If we still think that Electra is justified by Sophocles, let us notice that she directs Aegisthus' body to be thrown to the dogs. This is, as all Greek students know, an outrage on religion and human decency, as the fifth century understood it, and is described as such by Sophocles himself in the *Ajax* and the *Antigone*. It happened at times, it is true, during the Peloponnesian War, and it is always regarded as barbaric.

No, this is no justification of Electra. Sophocles is often concerned with the power of hate—in the *Ajax*, the *Trachiniae*, the *Philoctetes*, and the *Oedipus at Colonus*. The *Electra* is a play about the power of hate and misery bred in a particular personality which finally seems to lose the natural power to create. The girl cannot live spontane-ously. Her life is a series of responses—of hate for ill treatment, of love and hope for the fulfilment of revenge. The events of the years gone by shape everything else, to the elimination of any sense of the immediate present, except as the continuation of the past. The *Electra* is perhaps the best-constructed and most unpleasant play that Sophocles wrote. The tightness and cogency of the plot go to-gether with the absence of nobility and magnitude in the chief char-acter in a way which never occurred again in the extant plays. For sheer clarity and power, its author probably never improved on it.

ELECTRA

CHARACTERS

Paedagogus, the Old Servant Who Looked after Orestes when a Boy

Orestes, Son of Agamemnon, Murdered King of Mycenae

Electra, Daughter of Agamemnon

Chorus of Women of Mycenae

Chrysothemis, Sister of Electra

Clytemnestra, Widow of Agamemnon and Wife of Aegisthus

Aegisthus, Usurping King of Mycenae

ELECTRA

SCENE: *Before the royal palace in Mycenae.*

Paedagogus
> Son of Agamemnon, once general at Troy,
> now you are here, now you can see it all,
> all that your heart has always longed for.
> This is old Argos of your yearning, the grove
> of Inachus' gadfly-haunted daughter.
> And here, Orestes, is the Lycean market place
> of the wolf-killing God. Here on the left
> the famous temple of Hera. Where we have come now,
> believe your eyes, see golden Mycenae,
> and here the death-heavy house of the Pelopidae.   10
>
> Once on a time, your father's murder fresh,
> I took you from this house, received you from the hand
> of your sister, whose blood and father were yours.
> I saved you then. I have raised you from that day
> to this moment of your manhood to be the avenger
> of that father done to death. Orestes, now,
> and you, Pylades, dearest friend, take counsel
> quickly on what to do. Already the sunlight,
> brightening, stirs dawning bird song into clearness,
> and the black, kindly night of stars is gone.
> Before a man leaves his house, sets foot on the path,   20
> let us hold our parley. We are where
> we must not shrink. It is high time for action.

Orestes
> Dearest of servants:
> very plain are the signs you show of your nobility
> toward me. It is so with a horse of breeding.
> Even in old age, hard conditions
> do not break his spirit. His ears are still erect.

So it is with you. You urge me, and yourself
follow among the first. Therefore, I will make plain
all my determinations. Give keen ear   30
to what I say, and where I miss the mark
of what I should, correct me.

When I came to Pytho's place of prophecy
to learn to win revenge
for my father's murder on those that did that murder,
Phoebus spoke to me the words I tell you now:
"Take not spear nor shield nor host;
go yourself, and craft of hand
be yours to kill, with justice but with stealth."
Now we have heard the oracle together.
Go you into this house when occasion calls you.
Know all that is done there, and, knowing, report   40
clear news to us. You are old. It's a long time.
They will never know you. They will not suspect you
with your gray silver hair. Here is your story.
You are a stranger coming from Phanoteus,
their Phocian friend, the greatest of their allies.
Tell them a sudden accident befell
Orestes, and he's dead. Swear it on oath.
Say in the Pythian games he was rolled
out of his chariot at high speed.
That is your story now.   50

We shall go first to my father's grave
and crown it, as he bade us, with libations
and with cuttings from my thick, luxuriant hair.
And then we shall come here again
and in our hands a carved bronze-sided urn,
the urn that you know I hid here in the bushes.
By these means we shall bring the pleasant news
with our tale of lies, that here is my body,
quite gone to ashes, charred and burned, before them.

For why should it irk me if I die in word
but in deed come through alive and win my glory?   60
To my thinking, no word is base when spoken with profit.
Before now I have seen wise men often
dying empty deaths as far as words reported them,
and then, when they have come to their homes again,
they have been honored more, even to the skies.
So in my case I venture to predict
that I who die according to this rumor
shall, like a blazing star, glare on my foes again.

Land of my father, Gods of my country,
welcome me, grant me success in my coming,
and you, too, house of my father;
as your purifier I have come,
in justice sent by the Gods.   70
Do not send me dishonored out of this country,
but rich from of old time, restorer of my house.
This is all that I have to say. Old man,
let it be yours to go and mind your task.
We two must go away. It is seasonable,
and seasonableness is greatest master of every act.

Electra (*from inside the house cries out*)
Ah! Ah!

Paedagogus
Inside the house some one of the servants,
I think, is crying.

Orestes
Might it not be   80
unfortunate Electra? Do you want us
to stay here and to listen to her cries?

Paedagogus
No. Nothing must come before we try
to carry out what Loxias has bidden us.
From there we must make our beginning,

pouring the lustral offerings for your father.
For that, I think, will bring us victory,
and mastery in our enterprise.

(Orestes and his friends withdraw; Electra emerges.)

Electra

O Holy Light
and air, copartner with light in earth's possession,
how many keening dirges,
how many plangent strokes
laid on the breast till the breast was bloody,   90
have you heard from me
when the darkling night withdrew?
And again in the house of my misery
my bed is witness to my all-night sorrowing
dirges for my unhappy father.
Him in the land of the foreigner
no murderous god of battles entertained.
But my mother and the man who shared her bed,
Aegisthus, split his head with a murderous ax,
like woodsmen with an oak tree.
For all this no pity was given him,   100
by any but me, no pity for your death,
father, so pitiful, so cruel.
But, for my part, I
will never cease my dirges and sorrowful laments,
as long as I have eyes to see
the twinkling light of the stars and this daylight.
So long, like a nightingale, robbed of her young,
here before the doors of what was my father's house
I shall cry out my sorrow for all the world to hear.

House of the Death God, house of Persephone,   110
Hermes of the Underworld, holy Curse,
Furies the Dread Ones, children of the Gods,
all ye who look upon those who die unjustly,
all ye who look upon the theft of a wife's love,

come all and help take vengeance for my father,
for my father's murder!
And send me my brother to my aid.
For alone to bear the burden I am no longer strong enough,
the burden of the grief that weighs against me.   120

Chorus

Electra, child of the wretchedest of mothers,
why with ceaseless lament do you waste away
sorrowing for one long dead,
Agamemnon, godlessly trapped
by deceits of your treacherous mother,
betrayed by her evil hand?
May evil be the end
of him that contrived the deed,
if I may lawfully say it!

Electra

True-hearted girls,
you have come to console me in my troubles.   130
I know, I understand what you say,
nothing of it escapes me.
But, all the same, I will not
leave my mourning for my poor father.
You whose love responds to mine in all ways,
suffer me my madness,
I entreat you.

Chorus

But from the all-receptive lake
of Death you shall not raise him,
groan and pray as you will.
If past the bounds of sense you dwell in grief   140
that is cureless, with sorrow unending,
you will only destroy yourself,
in a matter where the evil knows no deliverance.
It is only your discomfort.
Why do you seek it?

Electra

Simple indeed is the one
that forgets parents pitifully dead.
Suited rather to my heart
the bird of mourning
that "Itys, Itys" ever does lament,
the bird of crazy sorrow, Zeus's messenger.
And Niobe, that suffered all, you, too,   150
I count God
who weeps perpetually
in her rocky grave.

Chorus

Not alone to you, my child,
this burden of grief has come.
You exceed in your feeling far
those of your kin and blood.
See the life of Chrysothemis
and Iphianassa,
and that one whose manhood grows in secret,
sorrowing, a prince,   160
whom one day this famed land of noble Mycenae
shall welcome back, if God will bless his coming,
Orestes.

Electra

I have awaited him always
sadly, unweariedly,
till I'm past childbearing,
till I am past marriage,
always to my own ruin.
Wet with tears, I endure
an unending doom of misfortune.
But he has forgotten
what he has suffered, what he has known.
What message comes from him to me
that is not again belied?   170

Yes, he is always longing to come,
but he does not choose to come, for all his longing.

Chorus

Take heart, take heart, my child.
Still great above is Zeus,
who oversees all things in sovereign power.
Confide to him your overbitter wrath.
Chafe not overmuch against
the foes you hate, nor yet forget them quite,
for Time is a kindly God.
For neither he that lives
by Crisa's cattle-grazing shore,   180
the son of Agamemnon, will be heedless,
nor the God that rules by Acheron's waters.

Electra

But for me already the most of my life
has gone by without hope.
And I have no strength any more.
I am one wasted in childlessness,
with no loving husband for champion.
Like some dishonored foreigner,
I tenant my father's house in these ugly rags   190
and stand at a scanty table.

Chorus

Pitiful was the cry at the homecoming,
and pitiful, when on your father on his couch
the sharp biting stroke of the brazen ax
was driven home.
Craft was the contriver, passion the killer,
dreadfully begetting between them a Shape,
dreadful, whether divine or human,
was he that did this.   200

Electra

That day of all days that have ever been
most deeply my enemy.

O night, horrible burden
of that unspeakable banquet.
Shameful death that my father saw
dealt him by the hands of the two,
hands that took my own life captive,
betrayed, destroyed me utterly.
For these deeds may God in his greatness,
the Olympian one, grant punishment to match them.   210
And may they have no profit of their glory
who brought these actions to accomplishment.

Chorus

    Take heed you do not speak too far.
    Do you not see from what
    acts of yours you suffer as you do?
    To destruction self-inflicted
    you fall so shamefully.
    You have won for yourself
    superfluity of misfortune,
    breeding wars in your sullen soul
    evermore. You cannot fight
    such conflicts hand to hand, with mighty princes.   220

Electra

    Terrors compelled me,
    to terrors I was driven.
    I know it, I know my own spirit.
    With terrors around me, I will not hold back
    these mad cries of misery, so long as I live.
    For who, dear girls, who that thought right
    would believe there were suitable comforting
    words for me?
    Forbear, forbear, my comforters.
    These ills of mine shall be called cureless   230
    and never shall I give over my sorrow,
    and the number of my dirges none shall tell.

Chorus

>But only in good will to you I speak
>like some loyal mother, entreating
>not to breed sorrow from sorrow.

Electra

>What is the natural measure of my sorrow?
>Come, how when the dead are in question,
>can it be honorable to forget?
>In what human being is this instinctive?
>Never may I have honor of such,
>nor, if I dwell with any good thing,   240
>may I live at ease, by restraining
>the wings of shrill lament to my father's dishonor.
>For if he that is dead
>is earth and nothing,
>poorly lying,
>and they shall never in their turn
>pay death for death in justice,
>then shall all shame be dead
>and all men's piety.   250

Chorus

>My child, it was with both our interests at heart
>I came, both yours and mine. If what I say
>is wrong, have your own way. We will obey you.

Electra

>Women, I am ashamed if I appear
>to you too much the mourner with constant dirges.
>What I do, I must do. Pardon me. I ask you
>how else would any well-bred girl behave
>that saw her father's wrongs, as I have seen these,
>by day and night, always, on the increase
>and never a check?   260
>First there's my mother, yes, my mother, now become
>all hatred. Then in the house I live with those
>who murdered my father. I am their subject, and

whether I eat or go without depends
on them.
           What sort of days do you imagine
I spend, watching Aegisthus sitting
on my father's throne, watching him wear
my father's self-same robes, watching him
at the hearth where he killed him, pouring libations?   270
Watching the ultimate act of insult,
my father's murderer in my father's bed
with my wretched mother—if mother I should call her,
this woman that sleeps with him.
She is so daring that she paramours
this foul, polluted creature and fears no Fury.
No, as though laughing at what was done,
she has found out the day on which she killed
my father in her treachery, and on that day
has set a dancing festival and sacrifices   280
sheep, in monthly ritual, "to the Gods that saved her."
So within that house I see, to my wretchedness,
the accursed feast named in his honor.
I see it, moan, and waste away, lament—
but only to myself. I may not even cry
as much as my heart would have me.
For this woman, all nobility in words,
abuses me: "You hateful thing, God-hated,
are you the only one whose father is dead?
Is there no one else of human kind in mourning?   290
My curse upon you! May the Gods below
grant you from your present sorrows no release!"
Such is the tone of her insults, unless she hears
from someone of Orestes' coming. Then
she grows really wild and stands beside me shrieking:
"Are you too not responsible for this?
Is not this your doing, you who stole
Orestes from these hands of mine, conveying him
away? But you may be sure you will pay for it

and pay enough." She howls so, and nearby her
is her distinguished bridegroom, saying the same,   300
that utter dastard, mischief complete,
who makes his wars with women.
But I am waiting for Orestes' coming,
waiting forever for the one who will stop
all our wrongs. I wait and wait and die.
For his eternal going-to-do-something
destroys my hopes, possible and impossible.

In such a state, my friends, one cannot
be moderate and restrained nor pious either.
Evil is all around me, evil
is what I am compelled to practice.

Chorus

Tell me, as you talk like this, is Aegisthus here,   310
or is he gone from home?

Electra

Certainly, he's gone.
Do not imagine, if he were near, that I
would wander outside. Now he is on his estate.

Chorus

If so, I can talk with you with better heart.

Electra

For the present, he is away. What do you want?

Chorus

Tell me: what of your brother? Is he really coming
or hesitating? That is what I want to know.

Electra

He says he is—but does nothing of what he says.

Chorus

A man often hesitates when he does a big thing.   320

Electra

I did not hesitate when rescuing him.

Chorus

    Be easy.

    He's a true gentleman and will help his friends.

Electra

  I believe in him, or else had not lived so long.

Chorus

    Say no more now. I see your sister,

    blood of your blood, of the same father and mother,

    Chrysothemis, in her hands burial offerings,

    the usual sacrifice to the Gods below.

                     (Enter Chrysothemis, Electra's sister.)

Chrysothemis

    What have you come to say out of doors,

    sister? Will you never learn, in all this time,   330

    not to give way to your empty anger?

    Yet this much I know, and know my own heart, too,

    that I am sick at what I see, so that

    if I had strength, I would let them know how I feel.

    But under pain of punishment, I think,

    I must make my voyage with lowered sails,

    that I may not seem to do something and then prove

    ineffectual. But justice, justice,

    is not on my side but on yours. If I am

    to live and not as a prisoner, I must

    in all things listen to my lords.   340

Electra

  It is strange indeed that you who were born

  of our father should forget him

  and heed your mother. All these warnings

  of me you have learned from her. Nothing is your own.

  Now you must make your choice, one way or the other,

  either to be a fool

  or sensible—and to forget your friends.

  Here you are saying: "If I had the strength,

I would show my hatred of them!" You who, when I
did everything to take vengeance for my father,
never did a thing to help—yes, discouraged the doer.   350
Is not this cowardice on top of baseness?
Tell me, or let me tell you, what benefit
I would achieve by giving up my mourning?
Do I not live? Yes, I know, badly, but
for me enough. And I hurt them
and so give honor to the dead, if there is, there
in that other world, anything that brings pleasure.
But you who hate, you tell me, hate in word only
but in fact live with our father's murderers.

I tell you: never, not though they brought me your gifts
in which you now feel pride, would I yield to them.   360
Have your rich table and your abundant life.
All the food I need is the quiet of my conscience.
I do not want to win your honor.
nor would you if you were sound of mind. Now, when you could
be called the daughter of the best of fathers,
be called your mother's. Thus to most people prove base,
traitor to your dead father and your friends.

Chorus

    No anger, I entreat you. In the words of both
    there is value for both, if you, Electra, can   370
    follow her advice and she take yours.

Chrysothemis

    O ladies, I am used to her and her words.
    I never would have mentioned this, had not
    I learned of the greatest of misfortunes coming
    her way to put a stop to her long mourning.

Electra

    Tell me of your terror. If you can speak to me
    of something worse than this condition of mine,
    I'll not refuse it still.

Chrysothemis
Well, I shall tell you.

From what I learned—and if you don't give over
your present mourning—they will send you where   380
never a gleam of sun shall visit you.
You shall live out your life in an underground cave
and there bewail sorrows of the world outside.
With this in mind, reflect. And do not blame me
later when you are suffering.
Now is a good time to take thought.

Electra
So this is what they have decided to do with me.

Chrysothemis
Yes, this exactly, when Aegisthus comes home.

Electra
As far as this goes, let him come home soon.

Chrysothemis
Why such a prayer for evil, my poor darling?

Electra
That he may come—if he will do what you say.

Chrysothemis
Hoping that *what* may happen you? Are you crazy?   390

Electra
That I may get away from you all, as far as I can.

Chrysothemis
Have you no care of this, your present life?

Electra
Mine is indeed a fine life, to be envied.

Chrysothemis
It might be, if you could learn common sense.

Electra
Do not teach me falseness to those I love.

Chrysothemis

That, that is not what I teach, but to yield to authority.

Electra

Practice your flattery. This is not my way.

Chrysothemis

It is a good thing, though, not to fall through stupidity.

Electra

I shall fall, if I must, revenging my father.

Chrysothemis

My father will have pardon for me, I know.   400

Electra

These are words that the base may praise.

Chrysothemis

You will not heed me then? You will not agree?

Electra

No, certainly.
May I not yet be so empty-witted.

Chrysothemis

Then I must go on the errand I was bid.

Electra

Where are you going? To whom
bringing burnt offering?

Chrysothemis

My mother sent me with offerings for father's grave.

Electra

What are you saying? To her greatest enemy?

Chrysothemis

"Whom she has killed"—you would add.

Electra

Which of her friends persuaded her? Who thought of this?

Chrysothemis

    I think it was night terrors drove her to it.   410

Electra

    Gods of my father, now or never stand my friends!

Chrysothemis

    Why do "night terrors" make you confident?

Electra

    I'll tell you that when you tell me the dream.

Chrysothemis

    I cannot tell you much, only a little.

Electra

    Tell me it, all the same. Often this little
    has made or ruined men.

Chrysothemis

    There is a story that she saw my father,
    the father that was yours and mine, again
    coming to life, once more to live with her.
    He took and at the hearth planted the scepter   420
    which once he bore and now Aegisthus bears,
    and up from out the scepter foliage sprang
    luxuriantly, and shaded all the land
    of this Mycenae. This is what I heard
    from someone present when she told the Sun
    the nature of her dreams.
                     But beyond this
    I know no more, only that she sends me
    because of her fear. And, by the Gods, I pray you,
    the Gods that live in this country, listen to me
    and do not fall out of stupidity.
    For if you should reject me, she will come
    again to harry you with punishment.   430

Electra

    My dear one, not a morsel that you hold
    allow to touch that grave, no, nothing.

It would not be God's law nor pious that you
should offer to my father sacrifices
and lustral offerings from that enemy woman.
Throw them to the winds! Or hide them in deep hollowed
earth, somewhere where no particle of them
may ever reach my father where he lies.
But let them be stored up for her as treasures
below, against the day when *she* shall die.
I tell you, if she were not the most brazen   440
of all of womankind, would she have dared
to pour these enemy libations
over the body of the man she killed?
Consider if you think that the dead man,
as he lies in his grave, will welcome kindly
these offerings from her by whom he was robbed
of life and honor? By whom, mutilated?
And for her purification she wiped
the blood stains on his head? Can you believe
that these will prove for her a quittance offering?
No, no. You let them be. You cut a lock
out of your own hair, from the fringe and mine,
mine, too, his wretched daughter's. Such a small offering   450
yet all I have! Give it to him, this lustrous
lock of hair, and here, my girdle, unadorned.
Kneel then and pray that from that nether world
he may come, a friendly spirit, to our help
against his enemies. Pray that the boy Orestes
may live to fight and win against his enemies,
may live to set his foot upon them.
                                   And so
in days to come we shall be able to dress
this grave with richer hands than we can now.
I think, oh yes, I think that it was he
that thought to send this evil-boding dream   460
to her.
         Yet, sister, do yourself this service

and help me, too, and help the dearest of all,
our common father, that lies dead in the underworld.

Chorus

 The girl speaks well. And you, my dear,
 if you are wise, will follow her advice.

Chrysothemis

 I will do it. It is not reasonable for us two
 to squabble about what is just. We must haste to do something.
 But, my friends, if I attempt this, I must have your silence.
 If my mother hears of this, I am sure I shall rue   470
 indeed the attempt I shall make.

Chorus

 If I am not a distracted prophet
 and lacking in skill of judgment,
 Justice foreshadowing the event
 shall come, in her hands a just victory.
 Yes, she will come, my child, in vengeance
 and soon.
 Of that I was confident
 when I lately heard,   480
 of this dream of sweet savor.
 Your father, the king of the Greeks,
 has never forgotten,
 nor the ax of old,
 bronze-shod, double-toothed,
 which did him to death
 in shame and baseness.

 There shall come many-footed, many-handed,
 hidden in dreadful ambush,   490
 the bronze-shod Fury.
 Wicked indeed were they who were seized
 with a passion for a forbidden bed,
 for a marriage accursed, stained with murder.
 In the light of this, I am very sure

that never, never shall we see
such a portent draw near without hurt
to doers and partners in crime.
There are no prophecies for mortal men
in dreadful dreams and soothsayings
if this night vision come not,   500
well and truly to fulfilment.

Horsemanship of Pelops of old,
loaded with disaster,
how deadly you have proved
to this land!
For since the day that Myrtilus
fell asleep, sunk in the sea,
wrecked utterly with the unhappy
wreck of his golden carriage,   510
for never a moment since
has destruction and ruin
ever left this house.

(*Queen Clytemnestra enters from the palace.*)

Clytemnestra

It seems you are loose again, wandering about.
Aegisthus isn't here, who always restrains you
from going abroad and disgracing your family.
But now that he is away you pay no heed
to me, although there's many a one you have told   520
at length how brutally and how unjustly
I lord it over you, insulting
you and yours.
                    There is no insolence in myself,
but being abused by you so constantly
I give abuse again.
                    Your father, yes,
always your father. Nothing else is your pretext—
the death he got from me. From me. I know it,
well. There is no denial in me. Justice,

Justice it was that took him, not I alone.
You would have served the cause of Justice if
you had been right-minded.
For this your father whom you always mourn,   530
alone of all the Greeks, had the brutality
to sacrifice your sister to the Gods,
although he had not toiled for her as I did,
the mother that bore her, he the begetter only.
Tell me, now, why he sacrificed her. Was it
for the sake of the Greeks?

They had no share in my daughter to let them kill her.
Was it for Menelaus' sake, his brother,
that he killed my child? And shall he not then pay for it?
Had not this Menelaus two children who
ought to have died rather than mine? It was their parents   540
for whose sake all the Greeks set sail for Troy.
Or had the God of Death some longing to feast
on my children rather than hers? Or had
that accursed father lost the love of mine
and felt it still for Menelaus' children?
This was the act of a father thoughtless
or with bad thoughts. That is how I see it
even if you differ with me.
                              The dead girl,
if she could speak, would bear me out.
I am not dismayed by all that has happened.
If you think me wicked, keep your righteous judgment   550
and blame your neighbors.

Electra
    This is one time you will not be able to say
    that the abuse I receive from you was provoked
    by something painful on my side.
                              But if
    you will allow me I will speak truthfully
    on behalf of the dead man and my dead sister.

Clytemnestra

Of course, I allow you. If you had always begun
our conversations so, you would not have been
so painful to listen to.

Electra

I will tell you, then.
You say you killed my father. What claim more shameful
than that, whether with justice or without it? 560
But I'll maintain that it was not with justice
you killed him, but the seduction of that bad man,
with whom you now are living, drew you to it.
Ask Artemis the Huntress what made her hold
the many winds in check at Aulis. Or
I'll tell you this. *You* dare not learn from her.

My father, as I hear, when at his sport,
started from his feet a horned dappled stag
within the Goddess' sanctuary. He
let fly and hit the deer and uttered some boast
about his killing of it. The daughter of Leto 570
was angry at this and therefore stayed the Greeks
in order that my father, to compensate
for the beast killed, might sacrifice his daughter.

Thus was her sacrifice—no other deliverance
for the army either homeward or toward Ilium.
He struggled and fought against it. Finally,
constrained, he killed her—not for Menelaus.
But if—I will plead in your own words—he had done so
for his brother's sake, is that any reason
why he should die at your hands? By what law?
If this is the law you lay down for men, take heed 580
you do not lay down for yourself ruin and repentance.
If we shall kill one in another's requital,
you would be the first to die, if you met with justice.

No. Think if the whole is not a mere excuse.
Please tell me for what cause you now commit
the ugliest of acts—in sleeping with him,
the murderer with whom you first conspired
to kill my father, and breed children to him, and
your former honorable children born   590
of honorable wedlock you drive out.
What grounds for praise shall I find in this? Will you say
that this, too, is retribution for your daughter?
If you say it, still your act is scandalous.
It isn't decent to marry with your enemies
even for a daughter's sake.

                                        But I may not
even rebuke you! What you always say
is that it is my mother I am reviling.
Mother! I do not count you mother of mine,
but rather a mistress. My life is wretched
because I live with multitudes of sufferings,
inflicted by yourself and your bedfellow.   600
But the other, he is away, he has escaped
your hand, though barely. Sad Orestes now
wears out his life in misery and exile.
Many a time you have accused me
of rearing him to be your murderer.
I would have done it if I could. Know that.
As far as that goes, you may publicly
proclaim me what you like—traitor, reviler,
a creature full of shamelessness.

                                        If I am
naturally skilled as such, I do no shame
to the nature of the mother that brought me forth.

Chorus
        I see she is angry, but whether it is in justice,   610
        I no longer see how I shall think of that.

                        « 148 »

Clytemnestra

    What need have *I* of thought in her regard
    who so insults her mother, when a grown woman?
    Don't you think she will go to any lengths, so shameless
    as she is?

Electra

          You may be sure I am ashamed,
    although you do not think it. I know why
    I act so wrongly, so unlike myself.
    The hate you feel for me and what you do
    compel me against my will to act as I do.   620
    For ugly deeds are taught by ugly deeds.

Clytemnestra

    O vile and shameless, I and my words and deeds
    give you too much talk.

Electra

    It is you who talk, not I. It is your deeds,
    and it is deeds invent the words.

Clytemnestra

    Now by the Lady Artemis you shall not escape
    the results of your behavior, when Aegisthus comes.

Electra

    You see? You let me say what I please, and then
    you are outraged. You do not know how to listen.

Clytemnestra

    Hold your peace at least. Allow me sacrifice,   630
    since I have permitted you to say all you will.

Electra

    I allow you, yes, I bid you, sacrifice.
    Do not blame my lips; for I will say no more.

Clytemnestra (*to the maid*)

    Come, do you lift them up, the offerings

of all the fruits of earth, that to this King here
I may offer my prayers for freedom from my fears.

(She speaks to the image of Apollo.)

Phoebus Protector, hear me, as I am,
although the word I speak is muted. Not among friends
is it spoken, nor may I unfold the whole
to the light while this girl stands beside me,   640
lest with her chattering tongue, wagging in malice,
she sow in all the city bad reports.
Yet hear me as I speak. So I will put it:
the dreams of double meaning I have seen
within this night, for them, Lycaean King,
grant what is good in them prosperous issue
but what is ill, turn it again upon
those that do us ill.
If there are some that from my present wealth
plot to expel me with their stratagems,
do not permit them. Let me live out my life,   650
just as my life is now, to the end uninjured,
controlling the house of Atreus and the throne,
living with those I love as I do now,
the good days on our side, and with such children
as do not hate me nor cause bitter pain.
These are my prayers, Lycaean Apollo, hear them
graciously. Grant to all of us what we ask.
For all the rest, although I am silent,
I know you are a God and know it all.
It is natural that the children of Zeus see all.

(Enter Paedagogus.)

Paedagogus

Foreign ladies, how may I know for certain,   660
is this the palace of the King Aegisthus?

Chorus

This is it, sir. Your own guess is correct.

« 150 »

Paedagogus

 Would I then be right in thinking this lady
 his wife? She has indeed a royal look.

Chorus

  Quite right. Here she is for you, herself.

Paedagogus

 Greetings, your Majesty. I come with news,
 pleasant news for you and Aegisthus and your friends.

Clytemnestra

 I welcome what you have said. I would like first
 to know who sent you here.

Paedagogus

      The Phocian,
 Phanoteus, charging me with a grave business.   670

Clytemnestra

 What is it, sir? Please tell me. I know well
 you come from a friend and will speak friendly words.

Paedagogus

 Orestes is dead. There it is, in one short word.

Electra

 O God, O God! This is the day I die.

Clytemnestra

 What is this you say, sir, what? Don't listen to her.

Paedagogus

 What I said and say now is "Orestes is dead."

Electra

 God help me, I am dead—I cannot live now.

Clytemnestra

 Leave her to herself. Sir, will you tell me the truth,
 in what way did he meet his death?

Paedagogus

      This
 I was sent to tell, and I will tell you it all.   680

He went to the glorious gathering that Greece holds
in honor of the Delphic Games, and when
he heard the herald's shrill proclamation
for the first contest—it was a running race—
he entered glorious, all men's eyes upon him.
His running was as good as his appearance.
He won the race and came out covered with honor.
There is much I could tell you, but I must tell it briefly.   690
I do not know a man of such achievement
or prowess. Know this one thing. In all the contests
the marshals announced, he won the prize, was cheered,
proclaimed the victor as "Argive by birth,
by name Orestes, son of the general
Agamemnon who once gathered the great Greek host."
So much for that. But when a God sends mischief,
not even the strong man may escape.
       Orestes,
when, the next day, at sunset, there was a race
for chariot teams, entered with many contestants.   700
There was one Achaean, one from Sparta, two
Libyans, masters in driving racing teams.
Orestes was the fifth among them. He
had as his team Thessalian mares. The sixth
was an Aetolian with young sorrel horses.
The seventh was a Magnesian, and the eighth
an Aenean, by race, with a white team.
The ninth competitor came from God-built Athens,
and then a Boeotian, ten chariots in all.
They stood in their allotted stations where   710
the appointed judges placed them. At the signal,
a brazen trumpet, they were off. The drivers
cheered their horses on, their hands vibrating the reins,
all together. All the course was filled
with the noise of rattling chariots. Clouds of dust
rose up. The mass of drivers, huddled together,
did not spare the goad as each one struggled

to put the nave of his wheel or the snorting mouths
of his horses past his rival, wheels and backs
of the foremost drivers all beslobbered with foam,   720
as the breath of the teams behind beat on them.
So far all chariots were uninjured. Then
the Aenean's hard-mouthed colts got out of hand
and bolted as they finished the sixth lap
and turned into the seventh. There they crashed
head on with the Barcaean. After that,
from this one accident, team crashed team
and overset each other. All the plain
of Crisa was full of wrecks. But the man from Athens,   730
a clever driver, saw what was happening, pulled
his horses out of the way and held them in check,
letting past the disordered mass of teams in the middle.
Orestes had been driving last and holding
his horses back, putting his trust in the finish.
But when he saw the Athenian left alone,
he sent a shrill cry through his good horses' ears
and set to catch him. The two drove level,
the poles were even. First one, now the other,
would push his horses' heads in front.   740
Orestes always drove tight at the corners
barely grazing the edge of the post with his wheel,
loosing his hold of the trace horse on his right
while he checked the near horse. In his other laps
the poor young man and his horses had come through safe.
But this time he let go of the left rein
as the horse was turning. Unaware, he struck the edge
of the pillar and broke his axle in the center.
He was himself thrown from the rails of the chariot
and tangled in the reins. As he fell, the horses
bolted wildly to the middle of the course.
When the crowd saw him fallen from his car,
they shuddered. "How young he was," "How gallant his deeds,"   750
and "How sadly he has ended," as they saw him

thrown earthward now, and then, tossing his legs
to the sky—until at last the grooms
with difficulty stopped the runaway team
and freed him, but so covered with blood that no one
of his friends could recognize the unhappy corpse.
They burned him on the pyre. Then men of Phocis
chosen for the task have brought here in a small urn
the lamentable ashes—all that is left
of this great frame, that he may have his grave   760
here in his father's country.
                         That is my story,
bitter as stories go, but for us who saw it,
greatest of all ill luck these eyes beheld.

Chorus
    Woe, woe. The ancient family
    of our lords has perished, it seems, root and branch.

Clytemnestra
    Zeus, what shall I say? Shall I say "good luck"
    or "terrible, but for the best"? Indeed,
    my state is terrible if I must save
    my life by the misfortunes of myself.

Paedagogus
    My lady, why does this story make you dejected?

Clytemnestra
    Mother and child! It is a strange relation.   770
    A mother cannot hate the child she bore
    even when injured by it.

Paedagogus
    Our coming here, it seems, then is to no purpose.

Clytemnestra
    Not to no purpose. How can you say "no purpose"?—
    if you have come with certain proofs of death
    of one who from my soul was sprung,
    but severed himself from my breast, from my nurture, who

became an exile and a foreigner;
who when he quitted this land, never saw me again;
who charged me with his father's murder, threatened
terrors against me. Neither night nor day   780
could I find solace in sleep. Time, supervisor,
conducted me to inevitable death.
But now, with this one day I am freed from fear
of her and him. She was the greater evil;
she lived with me, constantly draining
the very blood of life—now perhaps I'll have peace
from her threats. The light of day will come again.

Electra
My God! My God! Now must I mourn indeed
your death, Orestes, when your mother here
pours insults on you, dead. Can this be right?   790

Clytemnestra
Not right for you. But he is right as he is.

Electra
Hear, Nemesis, of the man that lately died!

Clytemnestra
She has heard those she should and done all well.

Electra
Insult us now. For now the luck is yours.

Clytemnestra
Will you not stop this, you and Orestes both?

Electra
We are stopped indeed. We cannot make you stop.

Clytemnestra (to the messenger)
Your coming will be worth much, sir, if you
have stopped my daughter's never ceasing clamor.

Paedagogus (with a feint at departure)
Well, I will go now, if all this is settled.

Clytemnestra

O no! I should do wrong to myself and to   800
the friend who sent you if I let you go.
Please go inside. Leave her out here to wail
the misfortunes of herself and those she loves.

(*Clytemnestra and the assumed messenger go into the house.*)

Electra

There's an unhappy mother for you! See
how agonized, how bitter, were the tears,
how terribly she sorrowed for her son
that met the death you heard of! No, I tell you,
she parted from us laughing. O my God!
Orestes darling, your death is my death.
By your passing you have torn away from my heart
whatever solitary hope still lingered   810
that you would live and come some day to avenge
your father and my miserable self.
But now where should I turn? I am alone,
having lost both you and my father. Back again
to be a slave among those I hate most
of all the world, my father's murderers!
Is this what is right for me?

                                 No, this I will not—
live with them any more. Here, at the gate
I will abandon myself to waste away
this life of mine, unloved. If they're displeased,
let someone kill me, someone that lives within.   820
Death is a favor to me, life an agony.
I have no wish for life.

Chorus

Where are Zeus's thunderbolts?
Where is the glowing sun?
If they see this and hide it
and hold their peace?

Electra (*cries out*)
  Oh!

Chorus
    Why do you cry, child?

Electra (*cries again*)
  Oh!

Chorus
    Speak no great word.   830

Electra
  You will destroy me.

Chorus
    How?

Electra
  If you suggest a hope
  when all is plain, when they are all gone
  to the house of Death, and when I waste
  my life away, you tread me further down.

Chorus
    King Amphiaraus, as I know,
    was caught in woman's golden snares
    and now beneath the earth
    reigns over all the spirits there.

Electra
  Oh! Oh!   840

Chorus
    Alas indeed, for pitiably

Electra
                            he died.

Chorus
    Yes.

Electra
  I know, I know. For him in sorrow
  there came a deliverer.

None such for me. For one there was,
but he is gone, ravished by death.

Chorus

Unhappy girl, unhappiness is yours!

Electra

I bear you witness with full knowledge.   850
Knowledge too full, bred of a life,
the crowded months surging with horrors
many and dreadful!

Chorus

We know what you mean.

Electra

So do not then, I pray you,
divert my thoughts to where . . .

Chorus

What do you mean?

Electra

. . . there is no hope, no kinsfolk,
and none among the nobles that will help.

Chorus

Death is the common lot of death-born men.   860

Electra

Yes, but to meet it so,
as he did, poor darling,
tangled in the leather reins,
among the wild competing hoofs.

Chorus

None can guess whence death will come.

Electra

True indeed. He is now a stranger
that was hidden in earth, by no hand of mine,
knew no grave I gave him,
knew no keening from me.   870

(Enter Chrysothemis.)

Chrysothemis
> My darling,
> I am so glad, I have run here in haste,
> regardless of propriety. I bring you
> happiness and a relief from all
> the troubles you have had and sorrowed for.

Electra
> Where could you find a cure—and who are you
> to find it—for my troubles which know no cure?

Chrysothemis
> We have Orestes here among us—that is
> my news for you—as plain as you see myself.

Electra
> Are you mad, poor girl, or can it be you laugh
> at what are your own troubles as well as mine?   880

Chrysothemis
> I swear by our father's hearth. It is not in mockery
> I speak. He is here in person with us.

Electra
> Ah!
> Wretched girl! Who told you this that you believed him,
> too credulous?

Chrysothemis
> My own eyes were the evidence
> for what I saw, and no one else.

Electra
> Poor thing!
> Poor thing! What proof was there to see? What did you
> see that has set your heart incurably
> afire?

Chrysothemis
> I pray you, hear me by the Gods,
> and having heard me, call me sane or foolish.   890

Electra

Tell me, then, if the story gives you pleasure.

Chrysothemis

Yes, I will tell you all I saw.
When I came to our father's ancient grave,
I saw that from the very top of the mound
newly spilled rills of milk were flowing. Round
the coffin was a wreath of all the flowers
that grow. I saw in wonder, looked about
for someone who would be near me. When I saw
that all was quiet, I approached the grave.   900
At the top of the pyre there was a lock of hair;
as soon as I saw that, something jumped within me
at the familiar sight. I know I saw
the token of my dearest, loved Orestes.
I took it in my hands, never saying a word
for fear of saying what would be ill-omened,
but with my joy my eyes were filled with tears.
Both then and now I know with certainty
this offering could come from him alone.
Whom else could this concern, save you and me?
I did not do it, I know, and neither did you.   910
How could you? For you cannot leave this house,
even to pray, but they will punish you for it.
Nor can it be our mother. She is not inclined
to do such things, nor, doing them, to be secret.
These offerings at the grave must be Orestes'.
Darling, take heart. It is not always the same
Genius that stands by the same people. Till now
he was hateful to us. But now perhaps
this day will seal the promise of much good.

Electra

Oh, how I have been pitying you for your folly!

Chrysothemis

What is this? Do I not say what is to your liking?   920

Electra

You do not know where you are, nor where your thoughts are.

Chrysothemis

Why should I not have knowledge of what I saw?

Electra

He is dead, my dear. Your rescue at his hands
is dead along with him. Look to him no more.

Chrysothemis

Alas! From whom on earth did you hear this?

Electra

From one that was near to him, when he was dying.

Chrysothemis

Where is he then? I am lost in wonderment.

Electra

In the house. He is our mother's welcome guest.

Chrysothemis

Alas again! But who then would have placed   930
these many offerings on our father's tomb?

Electra

I think perhaps that someone put them there
as a remembrance of the dead Orestes.

Chrysothemis

Unlucky I! I was so happy coming,
hurrying to bring my news to you, not knowing
what misery we were plunged in. Now when I've come,
I find both our old sorrow and the new.

Electra

That is how you see it. But now listen to me,
and you can relieve the suffering that weighs on us.

Chrysothemis

How can I bring the dead to life again?   940

Electra

This is not what I mean. I am no such fool.

Chrysothemis

    What do you bid me do, of which I am capable?

Electra

    To have the courage to follow my counsel.

Chrysothemis

    If I can help at all, I will not refuse.

Electra

    Look: there is no success without hardship.

Chrysothemis

    I see. As far as my strength goes, I will help.

Electra

    Hear me tell you, then, the plans that I have laid.
    Friends to stand by and help us we have none—
    nowhere—you know that quite as well as I.
    Death has taken them and robbed us. We alone,   950
    the two of us, are left.
    While I still heard my brother flourished,
    alive, I had my hopes he would still come,
    some day, to avenge the murder of his father.
    But now that he's no more, I look to you,
    that you should not draw back from helping me,
    your true-born sister, kill our father's murderer
    that killed him with his own hand—Aegisthus.
    There is nothing I should now conceal from you.
    What are you waiting for, that you are hesitant?
    What hope do you look to, that is still standing?
    Now you must sorrow for the loss of fortune   960
    that was our father's. Now you must grieve
    that you have already so many years
    without a marriage and a husband. Do not
    hope you will get them now. For Aegisthus
    is not such a fool to suffer to grow up
    children of you and me, clearly to harm him.
    But if you follow my plans,

first, you will win from that dead father, gone
to the underworld, and from our brother with him,
the recognition of your piety.
And, secondly, as you were born to freedom,   970
so in the days to come you will be called free
and find a marriage worthy of you; for all
love to look to the noble.
Do you not see how great a reputation
you will win yourself and me by doing this?
For who of citizens and foreigners
that sees us will not welcome us with praise:
"These are two sisters, friends. Look on them well.
They saved their father's house when their foes
were riding high, stood champions against murder,
sparing not to risk their lives upon the venture.   980
Therefore, we all should love them, all revere them,
and all at feasts and public ceremonies
honor these two girls for their bravery."

This is what everyone will say of us,
in life and death, to our undying fame.
My dear one, hear me. Take sides with your father
and with your brother. Give me deliverance
from what I suffer. Deliver yourself, knowing this:
life on base terms, for the nobly born, is base.

Chorus

    In such concerns forethought is an ally   990
    to the one that gives, and her that gets advice.

Chrysothemis

    Ladies, before she spoke, if she had good sense,
    she would have held to prudence, as she has not.

                              (*To Electra.*)

    To what can you look to give you confidence
    to arm yourself and call on me to help?
    Can you not see? You are a woman—no man.

Your physical strength is less than is your enemies'!
Their Genius, day by day, grows luckier
while ours declines and comes to nothingness. 1000
Who is there, plotting to kill such a man
as this Aegisthus, would come off unhurt?
We two are now in trouble. Look to it that
we do not get ourselves trouble still worse
if someone hears what you have said.
There is no gain for us, not the slightest help,
to win a noble reputation if
the way to it lies by dishonorable death.
For death is not the worst but when one wants
to die and cannot even have that death.
I beg of you, before you utterly
destroy us and exterminate our family, 1010
check your temper. All that you have said to me
shall be, for my part, unspoken, unfulfilled.
Be sensible, you, and, at long last, being weaker,
learn to give in to those that have the strength.

Chorus
> Give heed to her. No greater gain for man
> than the possession of a sensible mind!

Electra
> You have said nothing unexpected. Well
> I knew you would reject what I proposed.
> The deed must then be done by my own hand
> alone. For I will not leave it unfulfilled. 1020

Chrysothemis
> Ah!
> I would you had felt so when our father died.
> You would have carried all before you.

Electra
> I was the same in nature, weaker in judgment.

Chrysothemis
> Practice to keep that judgment through your life.

Electra

That is advice which means you will not help me.

Chrysothemis

Yes—for the effort itself implies disaster.

Electra

I envy you your "judgment," hate your cowardice.

Chrysothemis

I will be equally patient when you praise me.

Electra

That you will never experience from me.

Chrysothemis

There's a long future to determine that.   1030

Electra

Begone; for there's no help in you for me.

Chrysothemis

There is, but there's no learning it in you.

Electra

Go and tell all this story to your mother.

Chrysothemis

On my side there is no such hatred as that.

Electra

Understand, at least, how you dishonor me.

Chrysothemis

There is no dishonor, only forethought for you.

Electra

Must I then follow *your* conception of justice?

Chrysothemis

You will think it *ours*, when you come to your senses.

Electra

It is terrible to speak well and be wrong.

Chrysothemis

A very proper description of yourself.   1040

Electra

What! Do you not think that I say what I do with justice?

Chrysothemis

There are times when even justice brings harm with it.

Electra

These are laws by which I would not wish to live.

Chrysothemis

If you made your attempt, you would find that I was right.

Electra

Yes, I will make it. You will not frighten me.

Chrysothemis

Are you sure now? You will not think again?

Electra

No enemy is worse than bad advice.

Chrysothemis

You cannot agree with any of what I say?

Electra

I have made my mind up—and not of yesterday.

Chrysothemis

I will go away then. You cannot bring yourself   1050
to find my words right, nor I your disposition.

Electra

Go then. I will never call you back,
not though you long for it. It would be utter
folly to make so hopeless an attempt.

Chrysothemis

Well, if you think that you are right, go on
thinking so. When you are deep in trouble, then
you may agree with what I said.

Chorus

We see above our heads the birds,
true in their wisdom,

caring for the livelihood   1060
of those that gave them life and sustenance.
Why do we not pay our debts so?
By Zeus of the Lightning Bolt,
by Themis, Dweller in Heaven,
not long shall they go unpunished.
O Voice that goes to the dead below,
carry piteous accents,
to the Atridae in the underworld,
and tell of wrongs untouched
by joy of the dance.

Tell them that now their house is sick,   1070
tell them that their two children
fight and struggle, that they cannot
any more live in harmony together.
Electra, betrayed, alone,
is down in the waves of sorrow,
constantly bewailing her father's fate,
like the nightingale lamenting.
She takes no thought of death;
she is ready to leave the light
if only she can kill
the two Furies of her house.
Was there ever one so noble   1080
born of a noble house?

None of the good will choose to live
basely, if so living
they cloud their renown and die nameless.
O my child, my child, even so you
have chosen the common lot of mourning,
have rejected dishonor,
to win at once two reputations
as wise and best of daughters.

I pray that your life may be lifted high   1090

over your foes,
in wealth and power as much as now
you lie beneath their hand.
For I have found you in distress
but winning the highest prize
by piety toward Zeus
for observance of nature's greatest laws.

Orestes (*disguised as a Phocian countryman*)
   I wonder, ladies, if we were directed right
   and have come to the destination that we sought?

Chorus
   What do you seek? And what do you want here?   1100

Orestes
   I have asked all the way here where Aegisthus lives.

Chorus
   You have arrived and need not blame your guides.

Orestes
   Would some one of you be so kind to tell
   the household we have come, a welcome company?

Chorus
   This lady, nearest you, will bear the message.

Orestes
   Then, lady, will you signify within
   that certain men of Phocis seek Aegisthus.

Electra
   O God, O God, are these the certain proofs
   you bring of rumors we had before you came?

Orestes
   I do not know about rumor. Old Strophius sent me   1110
   here to bring news about Orestes.

Electra
   What is it, sir? How fear steals over me!

Orestes

We have the small remains of him in this urn,
this little urn you see us carrying.

Electra

Alas, Alas! This is it indeed, all clear.
Here is my sorrow visible, before me.

Orestes

If you are one that sorrows for Orestes
and his troubles, know this urn contains his body.

Electra

Sir, give it to me, by the Gods. If he
is hidden in this urn—give it into my hands,   1120
that I may keen and cry lament together
for myself and all my race with these ashes here.

Orestes (speaking to his men)

Bring it and give it to her, whoever she is.
It is not in enmity she asks for it.
One of his friends perhaps, or of his blood.

Electra (speaking to the urn)

Oh, all there is for memory of my love,
my most loved in the world, all that is left
of live Orestes, oh, how differently
from how I sent you forth, how differently
from what I hoped, do I receive you home.
Now all I hold is nothingness,
but you were brilliant when I sent you forth.   1130
Would that you had left life before I sent you
abroad to a foreign country, when I stole you
with these two hands, saved you from being murdered.
Then on that very day you would have died,
have lain there and have found your share,
your common portion, of your father's grave.
Now far from home, an exile, on alien soil

without your sister near, you died unhappily.
I did not, to my sorrow, wash you with
the hands that loved you, did not lift you up,
as was my right, a weight of misery,   1140
to the fierce blaze of the pyre. The hands of strangers
gave you due rites, and so you come again,
a tiny weight inclosed in tiny vessel.
Alas for all my nursing of old days,
so constant—all for nothing—which I gave you;
my joy was in the trouble of it. For never
were you your mother's love as much as mine.
None was your nurse but I within that household.
You called me always "sister." Now in one day
all that is gone—for you are dead. All, all
you have snatched with you in your going, like   1150
a hurricane. Our father is dead and gone.
I am dead in you; and you are dead yourself.
Our enemies laugh. Frantic with joy, she grows,
mother, no mother, whom you promised me,
in secret messages so often, you
would come to punish. This, all this, the Genius,
the unlucky Genius of yourself and me,
has stolen away and sent you back to me,
instead of the form I loved, only your dust
and idle shade. Alas! Alas!

      (*She takes up an attitude of formalized mourning by the urn.*)
O body pitiable! Alas!   1160
O saddest journey that you went, my love,
and so have ended me! Alas!
O brother, loved one, you have ended me.
Therefore, receive me to your habitation,
nothing to nothing, that with you below
I may dwell from now on. When you were on earth,
I shared all with you equally. Now I claim
in death no less to share a grave with you.
The dead, I see, no longer suffer pain.   1170

Chorus

>Think, Electra, your father was mortal,
>and mortal was Orestes. Do not sorrow too much.
>This is a debt that all of us must pay.

Orestes

>Ah!
>What shall I say? What words can I use, perplexed?
>I am no longer master of my tongue.

Electra

>What ails you? What is the meaning of your words?

Orestes

>Is this the distinguished beauty, Electra?

Electra

>   Yes.
>A miserable enough Electra, truly.

Orestes

>Alas for this most lamentable event!

Electra

>Is it for me, sir, you are sorrowing?   1180

Orestes

>Form cruelly and godlessly abused!

Electra

>None other than myself must be the subject
>of your ill-omened words, sir.

Orestes

>   O, alas!
>For your life without husband or happiness!

Electra

>Why do you look at me so, sir? Why lament?

Orestes

>How little then I knew of my own sorrows!

Electra

>In what of all that was said did you find this out?

Orestes

So great, so sore, I see your sufferings.

Electra

It's little of my suffering that you see.

Orestes

How can there be things worse than those I see?

Electra

Because I live with those that murdered him.   1190

Orestes

Murderers? And whose? Where is the guilt you hint at?

Electra

My father's murderers. I am their slave perforce.

Orestes

Who is it that forces you to such subjection?

Electra

She is called my mother—but like a mother in nothing.

Orestes

How does she force you? Hardship or violence?

Electra

With violence and hardship and all ills.

Orestes

You have none to help you or to hinder her?

Electra

No. There was one. You have shown me his dust.

Orestes

Poor girl! When I look at you, how I pity you.

Electra

Then you are the only one that ever pitied me.   1200

Orestes

Yes. I alone came here and felt your pain.

Electra

You haven't come as, in some way, our kinsman?

Orestes

I will tell—if (*pointing to the Chorus*) I may speak here among
friends.

Electra

Yes, friends indeed. You may speak quite freely.

Orestes

Give up this urn then, and you shall know all.

Electra

Don't take it from me, stranger—by the Gods!

Orestes

Do what I bid you. You will not be wrong.

Electra

By your beard! Do not rob me of what I love most!

Orestes

I will not let you have it.

Electra

O Orestes!

Alas, if I may not even give you burial!   1210

Orestes

No words of ill omen! You have no right to mourn.

Electra

Have I no right to mourn for my dead brother?

Orestes

You have no right to call him by that name.

Electra

Am I then so dishonored in his sight?

Orestes

No one dishonors you. Mourning is not for you.

Electra

It is—if I hold Orestes' body here.

Orestes

No body of Orestes—except in fiction.

Electra

Where is the poor boy buried then?

Orestes

Nowhere.
There is no grave for living men.

Electra

How, boy,
What do you mean?

Orestes

Nothing that is untrue.   1220

Electra

Is he alive then?

Orestes

Yes, if I am living.

Electra

And are you he?

Orestes

Look at this signet ring
that was our father's, and know if I speak true.

Electra

O happiest light!

Orestes

Happiest I say, too.

Electra

Voice, have you come?

Orestes

Hear it from no other voice.

Electra

Do my arms hold you?

Orestes

Never again to part.

Electra (to the Chorus)
> Dearest of women, fellow citizens,
> here is Orestes, that was dead in craft,
> and now by craft restored to life again.

Chorus
> We see, my child, and at your happy fortune   1230
> a tear of gladness trickles from our eyes.

Electra
> Child of the body that I loved the best,
> at last you have come,
> you have come, you have found, you have known those you
>   yearned for.

Orestes
> Yes, I have come.
> But bide your time in silence.

Electra
> Why?

Orestes
> Silence is better, that none inside may hear.

Electra
> No, by Artemis, ever virgin.
> *That* I will never stoop to fear—
> the women inside there,   1240
> always a vain burden on the earth.

Orestes
> Yes, but consider that in women too
> there lives a warlike spirit. You have proof of it.

Electra
> Alas, indeed.
> You have awakened my sorrow no cloud can dim,
> no expiation wash away,
> no forgetfulness overcome,
> no measure can fit,
> in all its frightfulness.

1250

Orestes

    I know that too. But when you may speak freely,
    then is the time to remember what was done.

Electra

    Every moment, every moment of all time
    would fit justly for my complaints.
    For hardly now are my lips free of restraint.

Orestes

    And I agree. Therefore, hold fast your freedom.

Electra

    By doing what?

Orestes

            Where there is no occasion,
    do not choose to talk too much.

Electra

    Who could find a fit bargain   1260
    of words for that silence,
    now you have appeared?
    Past hope, past calculation,
    I see you.

Orestes

    You see me when the Gods moved me to come.

Electra

    You tell me then of a grace surpassing
    what I knew before, if in very truth
    the Gods have given you to this house.
    This I count an action divine.   1270

Orestes

    Indeed, I hesitate to check your joy;
    only I fear your pleasure may be too great.

Electra

    Orestes, you have come at last,
    have made the journey worth all the world to me,

have come before me at last.
Now that I see you
after so much sorrow,
do not, I beg you—

Orestes

What should I not do?

Electra

Do not deprive me
of the joy of seeing your face.

Orestes

I would be angry if I saw another
trying to take me from you.

Electra

You agree?

Orestes

Yes.   1280

Electra

My dear one, I have heard you speaking,
the voice I never hoped to hear.
Till now I have held my rage speechless;
I did not cry out when I heard bad news.
But now I have you. You have come,
your darling face before me
that even in suffering I never forgot.

Orestes

Spare me all superfluity of speech.
Tell me not how my mother is villainous,
nor how Aegisthus drains my father's wealth   1290
by luxury or waste. Words about this
will shorten time and opportunity.
But tell me what we need for the present moment,
how openly or hidden we may make
this coming of ours a check for mocking foes.
Take care, you, that our mother may not discover you
by your radiant face, when we two go inside.

Groan as for my destruction, emptily
described in words. For when we have reached success,
then you may freely show your joy, and laugh.   1300

Electra

Brother, your pleasure shall be mine. These joys
I have from you. They are not mine to own.
To grieve you, though it were ever so little,
I would not buy a great good for myself.
If I did so, I would not properly
be servant to the Genius who attends us.
You know the situation. You have heard
Aegisthus is not at home, our mother is.
Do not be afraid that she will see my face
radiant with smiles. Our hatred is too old.   1310
I am too steeped in it. And since I have seen you,
my tears of joy will still run readily.
How can they cease when on the selfsame day
I have seen you dead and then again alive?
For me your coming is a miracle,
so that if my father should come back to life
I would think it no wonder but believe
I saw him. Since your coming is such for me,
lead as you will. Had I been all alone,
I would not have failed to win one of two things,   1320
a good deliverance or a good death for me.

Orestes

Hush, hush! I hear one of the people within
coming out.

Electra (still loudly to the servants of Orestes)
                        In with you, friends and guests,
more so, since what you are carrying in is that
which no one will reject there—nor be glad,
once he has got it.

Paedagogus (coming from inside)
                        Fools and madmen! No
concern for your own lives at all! No sense

to realize that you are not merely near
the deadliest danger, but in its very midst.   1330
If I had not, this while past, stood sentry here
at the door, your plans would now be in the house
before your bodies. I and I only
took the precautions. Have done once and for all
with your long speeches, your insatiate
cries of delight! And in with you at once.
As we are now, delay is ruinous.
It is high time to have done with our task.

Orestes

How shall I find everything inside?

Paedagogus

Well. There is no chance of your recognition.   1340

Orestes

You have announced my death, I understand.

Paedagogus

You are dead and gone—for all your being here.

Orestes

Were they glad of it? Or what did they say?

Paedagogus

I will tell you at the end. As things are now,
all on their side is well—even what is not so.

Electra

Brother, who is this man? I beg you, tell me.

Orestes

Do you not know him?

Electra

I cannot even guess.

Orestes

Do you not know him to whose hands you gave me?

Electra

What, this man?

Orestes

By his hands and by your forethought
I was conveyed away to Phocian country.   1350

Electra

Is this the man, alone among so many,
whom I found loyal when my father was murdered?

Orestes

This is he. There is no need for further questions.

Electra

O light most loved! O only rescuer
of Agamemnon's house, in what a shape
you come again! Are you indeed that other
who saved me and Orestes from many sorrows?
O most loved hands, service of feet most kind!
To think you have stood beside me for so long,
I not to know you, you to give no sign!
You killed me with your words while you had for me
most sweet reality. Bless you, my father,   1360
for in you I think I see my father. Bless you!
Within the selfsame day, of all mankind
I have most hated and loved you most.

Paedagogus

Enough, I think. As for the story
of the happenings in between, there are many days
and nights, as time comes round, to tell you all
clearly, Electra. But as you two stand here
I say to you: now is your chance to act.
Clytemnestra is alone. No man is there.
If you stop now, you will have others to fight   1370
more clever and more numerous than these.

Orestes

Pylades, we have time no longer for lengthy speeches.
We must get inside as quick as ever we can,
only first worshiping the ancestral Gods
whose statues stand beside the forecourt here.

(Exit Orestes.)

Electra (praying to the statue of Apollo)
 Apollo, Lord, give gracious ear to them
 and to me, too, that often made you offerings,
 out of such store as I had, with hand enriching.
 Lycean One, Apollo, now I pray,
 adore, entreat you on my knees, with all   1380
 the resources that I have, be kind to us,
 help us in the fulfilment of our plans
 and prove to all mankind the punishment
 the Gods exact for wickedness.

Chorus
 See how the War God approaches,
 breathing bloody vengeance, invincible.
 They have gone under the rooftree now,
 the pursuers of villainy,
 the hounds that none may escape.
 So that the dream that hung hauntingly   1390
 in my mind shall not lack fulfilment.
 Stealthy, stealthy, into the house,
 he goes, the champion of dead men,
 to his father's palace, rich from of old,
 with his hands on the tool of blood, new-whetted.
 Hermes, the child of Maia, conducts
 the crafty deed to its end, and delays not.

Electra
 Dear ladies, now is the moment that the men
 are finishing their work. Wait in silence.

Chorus
 What do you mean? What are they doing?

Electra

          She is preparing 1400
 the urn for burial, and they stand beside her.

Chorus
 Why have you hurried out here?

Electra

To watch

That Aegisthus does not come on them unawares.

Clytemnestra (cries from within the house)

House, O house
deserted by friends, full of killers!

Electra

Someone cries out, inside. Do you hear?

Chorus

What I hear is a terror to the ear.
I shudder at it.

Clytemnestra (cries again)

Oh! Oh!
Aegisthus, where are you?

Electra

Again, that cry!

Clytemnestra

My son, my son,
pity your mother!

1410

Electra

You had none for him,
nor for his father that begot him.

Chorus

City,

and miserable generation, now
the day-to-day pursuing fate is dying.

Clytemnestra

Oh! I am struck!

Electra

If you have strength—again!

Clytemnestra

Once more! Oh!

Electra

Would Aegisthus were with you!

Chorus

> The courses are being fulfilled;
> those under the earth are alive;
> men long dead draw from their killers
> blood to answer blood.   1420

> And here they come. The red hand reeks
> with War God's sacrifice. I cannot blame them.

Electra

  Orestes, how have you fared?

Orestes

                          In the house, all
  is well, if well Apollo prophesied.

Electra

  Is the wretch dead?

Orestes

                You need fear no more
  that your proud mother will dishonor you.

Chorus

> Stop! I can see Aegisthus clearly
> coming this way.

Electra

  Boys, back to the house!   1430

Orestes

  He is in our power!

Electra

  He walks from the suburb full of joy.

Chorus

> Back to the vestibule, quick as you can.
> You have done one part well. Here is the other.

Orestes

  Do not be concerned, we will do it.

Electra

Go

where you will, then.

Orestes

See, I am gone (*hiding himself*).

Electra

Leave what is here to me.

Chorus

A few words spoken softly in his ear
would be good, that unawares
he may rush to his fight where Justice   1440
will be his adversary.

Aegisthus

Which of you knows where the Phocians are?
I am told they are come here with news for me
that Orestes met his end in a chariot wreck.
You there, yes, I mean you, you, you—
you have been bold enough before, and I should think
it is you these news concern most and therefore
you will know best to tell me.

Electra

I know. Of course. Were it not so, I would
be outcast from what concerns my best beloved.

Aegisthus

Where are the strangers then? Tell me that.   1450

Electra

Inside. They have found their hostess very kind.

Aegisthus

And do they genuinely report his death?

Electra

Better than that. They have brought himself, not news.

Aegisthus

Can I then see the body in plain sight?

Electra

You can indeed. It is an ugly sight.

Aegisthus

What you say delights me—an unusual thing!

Electra

You may delight, if you can find it here.

Aegisthus

Silence now! (*to the servants*) I command you, open the doors
for Mycenaeans, Argives all, to see
that if there be a man whom empty hope   1460
has still puffed up, he may look on the dead
and so accept my bitting, so may shun
a forcible encounter with myself
and punishment to make him grow some sense.

Electra

I have done everything on my side. At long last
I have learned some sense, agreement with the stronger.

Aegisthus (*looking at the shrouded corpse*)

O Zeus, I see an image of what happened
not without envy of Gods. If that is something
I should not say, because of Nemesis,
I take it back. Draw all the covers from
his face that kinship at least may have due mourning.

Orestes

Touch it yourself. This body is not mine,   1470
it is only yours—to see and greet with love.

Aegisthus

True. I accept that. Will you call out
Clytemnestra if she is at home?

Orestes

                    She is near you.
You need not look elsewhere.

Aegisthus (as the face of Clytemnestra confronts him)
                              What do I see?

Orestes
    Something you fear? Do you not know the face?

Aegisthus
    Who are you that have driven us into the net
    in which this victim fell?

Orestes
                              Did you take so long
    to find that your names are all astray
    and those you call the dead are living?

Aegisthus
                              Ah!
    I understand. And you who speak to me   1480
    can only be Orestes.

Orestes
    Were you, so good a prophet, so long misled?

Aegisthus
    This is my end then. Let me say one word.

Electra
    Not one, not one word more,
    I beg you, brother. Do not draw out the talking.
    When men are in the middle of trouble, when one
    is on the point of death, how can time matter?
    Kill him as quickly as you can. And killing
    throw him out to find such burial as suit him
    out of our sights. This is the only thing
    that can bring me redemption from
    all my past sufferings.   1490

Orestes (to Aegisthus)
    In with you, then. It is not words that now
    are the issue, but your life.

Aegisthus

                         Why to the house?
Why do you need the dark if what you do
is fair? Why is your hand not ready to kill me?

Orestes

You are not to give orders. In where you killed him,
my father, so you may die in the same place!

Aegisthus

Must this house, by absolute necessity,
see the evils of the Pelopidae, now and to come?

Orestes

Yours it shall see, at least.
At least yours. There I am an excellent prophet.

Aegisthus

Your father did not have the skill you boast of.   1500

Orestes

Too many words! You are slow to take your road.
Go now.

Aegisthus

                   You lead the way.

Orestes

                                   No, you go first.

Aegisthus

Afraid that I'll escape you?

Orestes

No, but you shall not
die as you choose. I must take care that death
is bitter for you. Justice shall be taken
directly on all who act above the law—
justice by killing. So we would have less villains.

Chorus

O race of Atreus, how many sufferings
were yours before you came at last so hardly
to freedom, perfected by this day's deed.   1510

PHILOCTETES

Translated by David Grene

INTRODUCTION TO
PHILOCTETES

THE *Philoctetes* is the second-last play that Sophocles wrote. It probably came out in 409 B.C., and the last play, the *Oedipus at Colonus*, in 404, the year of Sophocles' death. Aristotle in the *Poetics* criticizes the *Philoctetes* for its happy ending, and many commentators since have been annoyed, or puzzled, or both by the solution of the play, which involves the God from the machine. Latterly, however, it has been more appreciated. There have been performances on the radio, and a surprising amount has been written about it, including a very interesting essay by Edmund Wilson in the *Wound and the Bow*. It is perhaps the most modern in feeling of all Sophocles' tragedies, and Sophocles is the most modern, the nearest to us, of the three Greek tragedians.

We may see the play simply as a duel between Philoctetes and Odysseus, with Neoptolemus as a pawn in the contest. But this play has a theme and a pattern which become deeper and more complicated, if we realize that in many of its aspects the story is the same as that of the *Oedipus at Colonus*. Each play, seen in the light of the other, makes more comprehensible Sophocles' tragic vision. Out of what personal suffering or vicarious experience he wrote this story twice in his last years, we shall never know. It is not only a preoccupation with the end of his life. With certain important differences the *Ajax*, written more than thirty years earlier than the *Philoctetes*, shows him thinking in the same way. Of course, each of these plays is individual in tone and character. What I mean is that, in both, the story is of a man offensive to his own society and banished by it, who, at last, must be reinstated and who becomes again miraculously potent, both alive and dead. And this story is the same in both plays in all its significant aspects.

Philoctetes is afflicted by some divine power without having committed a crime or being guilty of anything which the words "conscious guilt" mean, either to the fifth-century Greek or to ourselves.

He had unconsciously stumbled into a precinct or shrine of a God. Such shrines must not be thought of in the light of the Christian associations with the word. This was probably an unmarked and unfenced place, similar to the grove of the Eumenides in the *Oedipus at Colonus*. A snake—very often in Greece a symbol of a God's power—bit him in the foot and left him crippled. It is worth noting that Philoctetes' offense against the Gods is left at this. We are not allowed by the dramatist to speculate on any symbolic significance of his act of guilt or to construe it in any way as peculiar to Philoctetes. It is, in fact, an accident. He thus becomes burdened with the mark of God's resentment without any explanation for it humanly cogent either for himself or for others. The smell of his wound and his cries of agony render him so offensive to his comrades that he is marooned on a desert island for ten years, at the end of which time the Gods intervene to rescue him as mysteriously as they had injured him at the first. A glance at the Oedipus figure later and that of the Ajax in the earlier play shows a similar emphasis on the hero's innocence. It is true that Ajax is driven mad in the commission of an attempted murder against his generals, but Sophocles never tries to emphasize the matter of the murder afterward; it is only the performance of his act of frustration and misery by Ajax that we are likely to concern ourselves with.

Philoctetes is now an outcast from human sympathy but also the future conqueror of Troy. In both destruction and triumph, his lot does not make sense for ordinary men. This troubles them very little. They discarded him out of disgust at his affliction, when it looked as though God's hatred of him made that a safe course as well as a convenient one for themselves. Now that, with similar incomprehensibility, the divine purpose insists on the value of his bow and himself for the capture of Troy, they are prepared to restore him again to their society, particularly as the God has also arranged for his healing. In the *Philoctetes* Sophocles expresses what it feels like to be a man so isolated, so impersonally, so instrumentally used by his fellows.

The moment chosen is when the restoration to potency is near. Characteristically, Odysseus, who had marooned him originally and had taken advantage of Philoctetes when off his guard, plans to recapture him by similar strategic means. Neither time is he concerned to establish any human contact with the strange magical monster, so tormented and so honored by the non-human forces of the world. In this, Odysseus is blood-brother of Creon, who, in the *Oedipus at Colonus*, plays a similar role with the terrifying old beggar, Oedipus. In neither play does this cynical inhumanity have success. But neither are Philoctetes' brooding hatred and resentment allowed to have their way entirely. Here is where the role of Neoptolemus is important.

By trying to obey Odysseus, this boy comes to realize what cruelty is being inflicted on Philoctetes. So he undoes his offense and gives back the bow. However, when the deception is over and when the opportunity of healing and renown are offered Philoctetes again, by Neoptolemus this time, and as equal to equal, Philoctetes still refuses. The issue is clearly joined. Philoctetes' final refusal is the refusal of a man so wounded as to be unwilling to resume normal life itself because, with that life, will come new and unpredictable suffering. Better the old known pain, with the old known remedies, than the new hurt as unforeseeable as the future itself:

> It is not the sting of wrongs past,
> but what I must look for in wrongs to come.

This is all understandable, and, more than understandable, it claims our sympathy. But it is also irreconcilable with the vital principle which in anyone's life involves change and risk. It is easy for young Neoptolemus to face the future confidently. He has not yet been hurt enough to know what it feels like. Philoctetes' refusal is a great tragic human truth.

So Heracles is invoked not as an ordinary God from the machine but as the influence of a hero and old comrade, similarly injured, similarly restored, whose example must force Philoctetes to a step which will bring him healing and renown—but also more suffering. It is not that, as Aeschylus says, "out of suffering comes learning," but that only at the cost of suffering does life itself exist. As Philoctetes' final refusal is the mark of the play's truth to humanity, so is his final acquiescence in Heracles' order the mark of a truth to a universal principle, more imperative than humanity. But it is not the Philoctetes of the island, whom we have come to know so well, who goes to Troy with Odysseus and Neoptolemus. The significant part of that Philoctetes died, persisting to the end not to surrender his resentment and to risk new wrongs. This tragedy ends with his renewed refusal of Neoptolemus. What follows is what might well happen in the world as in the theater—the surrender of the individual life to the universal demands of life itself. As Hamlet must die and Fortinbras succeed, the new Philoctetes succeeds the old; but with the other Philoctetes of the island are buried all the years of wrong and of suffering and also the meaning that they had rendered to his agony.

CHARACTERS

Odysseus

Chorus of Sailors under the Command of Neoptolemus

The Spy Disguised as a Trader

Neoptolemus, Prince of Scyrus and Son of Achilles

Philoctetes

Heracles

PHILOCTETES

SCENE: *A lonely spot on the island of Lemnos. Enter Odysseus and Neoptolemus.*

Odysseus
    This is it; this Lemnos and its beach
    down to the sea that quite surrounds it; desolate,
    no one sets foot on it; there are no houses.
    This is where I marooned him long ago,
    the son of Poias, the Melian, his foot
    diseased and eaten away with running ulcers.

    Son of our greatest hero,
    son of Achilles, Neoptolemus,
    I tell you I had orders for what I did:
    my masters, the princes, bade me do it.

    We had no peace with him: at the holy festivals,
    we dared not touch the wine and meat; he screamed
    and groaned so, and those terrible cries of his
    brought ill luck on our celebrations; all
    the camp was haunted by him.   10

    Now is no time to talk to you of this,
    now is no time for long speeches.
    I am afraid that he may hear of my coming
    and ruin all my plans to take him.

    It is you who must help me with the rest. Look about
    and see where there might be a cave with two mouths.
    There are two niches to rest in, one in the sun
    when it is cold, the other a tunneled passage
    through which the breezes blow in summertime.

A man can sleep there and be cool. To the left,   20
a little, you may see a spring to drink at—
if it is still unchoked—go this way quietly,
see if he's there or somewhere else and signal.
Then I can tell you the rest. Listen:
I shall tell you. We will both do this thing.

Neoptolemus

What you speak of is near at hand, Odysseus.
I think I see such a cave.

Odysseus

Above or below? I cannot see it myself.

Neoptolemus

Above here, and no trace of a footpath.

Odysseus

See if he is housed within, asleep.   30

Neoptolemus

I see an empty hut, with no one there.

Odysseus

And nothing to keep house with?

Neoptolemus

A pallet bed, stuffed with leaves, to sleep on, for someone.

Odysseus

And nothing else? Nothing inside the house?

Neoptolemus

A cup, made of a single block, a poor
workman's contrivance. And some kindling, too.

Odysseus

It is his treasure house that you describe.

Neoptolemus

And look, some rags are drying in the sun
full of the oozing matter from a sore.

Odysseus

    Yes, certainly he lives here, even now   40
    is somewhere not far off. He cannot go far,
    sick as he is, lame cripple for so long.
    It's likely he has gone to search for food
    or somewhere that he knows there is a herb
    to ease his pain. Send your man here to watch,
    that he may not come upon me without warning.
    For he would rather take me than all the Greeks.

Neoptolemus

    Very well, then, the path will be watched.
    Go on with your story; tell me what you want.

Odysseus

    Son of Achilles,   50
    our coming here has a purpose; to it be loyal
    with more than with your body. If you should hear
    some strange new thing, unlike what you have heard
    before, still serve us; it was to serve you came here.

Neoptolemus

    What would you have me do?

Odysseus

                 Ensnare
    the soul of Philoctetes with your words.
    When he asks who you are and whence you came,
    say you are Achilles' son; you need not lie.
    Say you are sailing home, leaving the Greeks
    and all their fleet, in bitter hatred. Say
    that they had prayed you, urged you from your home,   60
    and swore that only with your help
    could Troy be taken. Yet when you came and asked,
    as by your right, to have your father's arms,
    Achilles' arms, they did not think you worthy
    but gave them to Odysseus. Say what you will
    against me; do not spare me anything.

Nothing of this will hurt me; if you will not
do this, you will bring sorrow on all the Greeks.
If this man's bow shall not be taken by us,
you cannot sack the town of Troy.

Perhaps you wonder why you can safely meet him,   70
why he would trust you and not me. Let me explain.
You have come here unforced, unpledged by oaths,
made no part of our earlier expedition.
The opposite is true in my own case;
at no point can I deny his charge.
If, when he sees me, Philoctetes
still has his bow, there is an end of me,
and you too, for my company would damn you.
For this you must sharpen your wits, to become a thief
of the arms no man has conquered.

I know, young man, it is not your natural bent
to say such things nor to contrive such mischief.   80
But the prize of victory is pleasant to win.
Bear up: another time we shall prove honest.
For one brief shameless portion of a day
give me yourself, and then for all the rest
you may be called most scrupulous of men.

Neoptolemus
Son of Laertes, what I dislike to hear
I hate to put in execution.
I have a natural antipathy
to get my ends by tricks and stratagems.
So, too, they say, my father was. Philoctetes
I will gladly fight and capture, bring him with us,   90
but not by treachery. Surely a one-legged man
cannot prevail against so many of us!
I recognize that I was sent with you
to follow your instructions. I am loath
to have you call me traitor. Still, my lord,

I would prefer even to fail with honor
than win by cheating.

Odysseus

You are a good man's son.
I was young, too, once, and then I had a tongue
very inactive and a doing hand.
Now as I go forth to the test, I see
that everywhere among the race of men
it is the tongue that wins and not the deed.

Neoptolemus

What do you bid me do, but to tell lies?   100

Odysseus

By craft I bid you take him, Philoctetes.

Neoptolemus

And why by craft rather than by persuasion?

Odysseus

He will not be persuaded; force will fail.

Neoptolemus

Has he such strength to give him confidence?

Odysseus

The arrows none may avoid, that carry death.

Neoptolemus

Then even to encounter him is not safe?

Odysseus

Not if you do not take him by craft, as I told you.

Neoptolemus

Do you not find it vile yourself, this lying?

Osysseus

Not if the lying brings our rescue with it.

Neoptolemus

How can a man not blush to say such things?   110

Odysseus

When one does something for gain, one need not blush.

Neoptolemus

What gain for me that he should come to Troy?

Odysseus

His weapons alone are destined to take Troy.

Neoptolemus

Then I shall not be, as was said, its conqueror?

Odysseus

Not you apart from them nor they from you.

Neoptolemus

They must be my quarry then, if this is so.

Odysseus

You will win a double prize if you do this.

Neoptolemus

What? If I know, I will do what you say.

Odysseus

You shall be called a wise man and a good.

Neoptolemus

Well, then I will do it, casting aside all shame.   120

Odysseus

You clearly recollect all I have told you?

Neoptolemus

Yes, now that I have understood it.

Odysseus

                                        Stay
and wait his coming here; I will go
that he may not spy my presence.
I will take with me to the ship this guard.
If you are too slow, I will send him back again,
disguise him as a sailor; Philoctetes
will never know him.
Whatever clever story he give you, then   130

fall in with it and use it as you need.
Now I will go to the ship and leave you in charge.
May Hermes, God of Craft, the Guide, for us
be guide indeed, and Victory and Athene,
the City Goddess, who preserves me ever.

(*Exit Odysseus.*)

Chorus

Sir, we are strangers, and this land is strange;
what shall we say and what conceal from this suspicious man?
Tell us.
For cunning that passes another's cunning
and a pre-eminent judgment lie with the prince,
in whose sovereign keeping is Zeus's holy scepter.   140
To you, young lord, all this has come,
all the power of your forefathers. Tell us now
what we must do to serve you.

Neoptolemus

Now—if you wish to see where he sleeps
on his crag at the edge—look, be not afraid.
But when the terrible wanderer returns,
be gone from the hut, but come to my beckoning.
Take your cues from me. Help when you can.

Chorus

Sir, this we have always done,   150
have kept a watchful eye over your safety.
But now
tell us what places he inhabits
and where he rests. It would not be amiss
for us to know this,
lest he attack us unawares.
Where does he live? Where does he rest?
What footpath does he follow? Is he in the house or not?

Neoptolemus

This, that you see, is his two-fronted house,
and he sleeps inside on the rock.   160

Chorus

Where is he gone, unhappy creature?

Neoptolemus

                      I am sure
he has gone to find food somewhere near here;
stumbling, lame, dragging along the path,
he is trying to shoot birds to prolong his miserable life.
This indeed, they say, is how he lives.
And no one comes near to cure him.

Chorus

Yes, for my part I pity him:
how unhappy, how utterly alone, always   170
he suffers the savagery of his illness
with no one to care for him,
with no friendly face near him,
but bewildered and distraught at each need as it comes.
God pity him, how has he kept a grip on life?

Woe to the contrivances of death-bound men,
woe to the unhappy generations of death-bound men
whose lives have known extremes!

Perhaps this man is as well born as any,   180
second to no son of an ancient house.
Yet now his life lacks everything,
and he makes his bed without neighbors
or with spotted shaggy beasts for neighbors.
His thoughts are set continually on pain and hunger.
He cries out in his wretchedness;
there is only a blabbering echo,
that comes from the distance speeding
from his bitter crying.   190

Neoptolemus

I am not surprised at any of this:
this is a God's doing, if I have any understanding.

These afflictions that have come upon him
are the work of Chryse, bitter of heart.
As for his present loneliness and suffering,
this, too, no doubt is part of the God's plan
that he may not bend against Troy
the divine invincible bow
until the time shall be fulfilled, at which it is decreed,
that Troy, as they say, shall fall to that bow.   200

Chorus

  Hush.

Neoptolemus

      What is it?

Chorus

          Hush! I hear a footfall,
footfall of a man that walks painfully.
Is it here?   Is it here?
I hear a voice, now I can hear it clearly,
voice of a man, crawling along the path,
hard put to it to move. It's far away,
but I can hear it; I can hear the sound well
the voice of a man wounded; it is quite clear now.

No more now, my son.   210

Neoptolemus

          No more of what?

Chorus

Your plots and plans. He is here, almost with us.
His is no cheerful marching to the pipe
like a shepherd with his flock.
No, a bitter cry.
He must have stumbled far down on the path,
and his moaning carried all the way here.
Or perhaps he stopped to look at the empty harbor,
for it was a bitter cry.

Philoctetes

    Men, who are you that have put in, rowing   220
    to a shore without houses or anchorage?
    What countrymen may I call you without offense?
    What is your people? Greeks, indeed, you seem
    in fashion of your clothing, dear to me.
    May I hear your voice? Do not be afraid
    or shrink from such as I am, grown a savage.
    I have been alone and very wretched,
    without friend or comrade, suffering a great deal.
    Take pity on me; speak to me; speak,
    speak if you come as friends.
                    No—answer me.   230
    If this is all
    that we can have from one another, speech,
    this, at least, we should have.

Neoptolemus

    Sir, for your questions, since you wish to know,
    know we are Greeks.

Philoctetes

                 Friendliest of tongues!
    That I should hear it spoken once again
    by such a man in such a place! My boy,
    who are you? Who has sent you here? What brought you?
    What impulse? What friendliest of winds?
    Tell me all this, that I know who you are.

Neoptolemus

    I am of Scyrus that the sea surrounds;
    I am sailing home. My name is Neoptolemus,   240
    Achilles' son. Now you know everything.

Philoctetes

    Son of a father—that I loved so dearly—
    and of a country that I loved, you that were reared
    by that old man Lycomedes, what kind of venture
    can have brought you to port here? Where did you sail from?

Neoptolemus

At present bound from Troy.

Philoctetes

From Troy? From Troy!
You did not sail with us to Troy at first.

Neoptolemus

You, then, are one that also had a share
in all that trouble?

Philoctetes

          Is it possible
you do not know me, boy, me whom you see here?

Neoptolemus

I never saw you before. How could I know you?   250

Philoctetes

You never heard my name then? Never a rumor
of all the wrongs I suffered, even to death?

Neoptolemus

I never knew a word of what you ask me.

Philoctetes

Surely I must be vile! God must have hated me
that never a word of me, of how I live here,
should have come home through all the land of Greece.
Yet they that outraged God casting me away
can hold their tongues and laugh! While my disease
always increases and grows worse. My boy,
you are Achilles' son. I that stand here   260
am one you may have heard of, as the master
of Heracles' arms. I am Philoctetes
the son of Poias. Those two generals
and Prince Odysseus of the Cephallenians
cast me ashore here to their shame, as lonely
as you can see me now, wasting with my sickness
as cruel as it is, caused by the murderous bite
of a viper mortally dangerous.

I was already bitten when we put in here
on my way from sea-encircled Chryse.   270
I tell you, boy, those men cast me away here
and ran and left me helpless. They were happy
when they saw that I had fallen asleep on the shore
in a rocky cave, after a rough passage.
They went away and left me with such rags—
and few enough of them—as one might give
an unfortunate beggar and a handful of food.
May God give them the like!
Think, boy, of that awakening when I awoke
and found them gone; think of the useless tears
and curses on myself when I saw the ships—
my ships, which I had once commanded—gone,
all gone, and not a man left on the island,   280
not one to help me or to lend a hand
when I was seized with my sickness, not a man!
In all I saw before me nothing but pain;
but of that a great abundance, boy.

Time came and went for me. In my tiny shelter
I must alone do everything for myself.
This bow of mine I used to shoot the birds
that filled my belly. I must drag my foot,
my cursed foot, to where the bolt
sped by the bow's thong had struck down a bird.   290
If I must drink, and it was winter time—
the water was frozen—I must break up firewood.
Again I crawled and miserably contrived
to do the work. Whenever I had no fire,
rubbing stone on stone I would at last produce
the spark that kept me still in life.
A roof for shelter, if only I have fire,
gives me everything but release from pain.

Boy, let me tell you of this island.   300
No sailor by his choice comes near it.

There is no anchorage, nor anywhere
that one can land, sell goods, be entertained.
Sensible men make no voyages here.
Yet now and then someone puts in. A stretch
of time as long as this allows much to happen.
When they have come here, boy, they pity me—
at least they say they do—and in their pity
they have given me scraps of food and cast-off clothes;
that other thing, when I dare mention it,   310
none of them will—bringing me home again.

It is nine years now that I have spent dying,
with hunger and pain feeding my insatiable
disease. That, boy, is what they have done to me,
the two Atridae, and that mighty Prince
Odysseus. May the Gods that live in heaven
grant that they pay, agony for my agony.

Chorus
    In this, I too resemble your other visitors.
    I pity you, son of Poias.

Neoptolemus
                    I am a witness,
    I also, of the truth of what you say.   320
    I know it is true. I have dealt with those villains,
    the two Atridae and the prince Odysseus.

Philoctetes
    Are you, as well as I, a sufferer
    and angry? Have you grounds against the Atridae?

Neoptolemus
    Give me the chance to gratify my anger
    with my hand some day!
    Then will Mycenae know and Sparta know
    that Scyrus, too, breeds soldiers.

Philoctetes
> Well said, boy!
You come to me with a great hate against them.
Because of what?

Neoptolemus
> I will tell you, Philoctetes—
for all that it hurts to tell it—
of how I came to Troy and what dishonor   330
they put upon me.
When fatefully Achilles came to die. . . .

Philoctetes
O stop! tell me no more. Let me understand
this first. Is he dead, Achilles, dead?

Neoptolemus
Yes, he is dead; no man his conqueror
but bested by a god, Phoebus the archer.

Philoctetes
Noble was he that killed and he that died.
Boy, I am at a loss which to do first,
ask for your story or to mourn for him.

Neoptolemus
God help you, I would think that your own sufferings
were quite enough without mourning for those of others.   340

Philoctetes
Yes, that is true. Again, tell me your story
of how they have insulted you.

Neoptolemus
> They came
for me, did great Odysseus and the man
that was my father's tutor, with a ship
wonderfully decked with ribbons. They had a story—
be it truth or lie—that it was God's decree
since he, my father, was dead, I and I only
should take Troy town.

This was their story. Sir, you can imagine
it did not take much time, when they had told it,   350
for me to embark with them.
Chiefly, you know, I was prompted by love of him,
the dead man. I had hope of seeing him
while still unburied. Alive I never had.
We had a favoring wind; on the second day
we touched Sigeion. As I disembarked,
all of the soldiers swarmed around me, blessed me,
swore that they saw Achilles alive again,
now gone from them forever. But he still lay
unburied. I, his mourning son, wept for him;   360
then, in a while, came to the two Atridae,
my friends, as it seemed right to do, and asked them
for my father's arms and all that he had else.
They needed brazen faces for their answer:
"Son of Achilles, all that your father had,
all else, is yours to take, but not his arms.
Another man now owns them, Laertes' son."
I burst into tears, jumped up, enraged,
cried out in my pain, "You scoundrels, did you dare
to give those arms that were mine to someone else   370
before I knew of it?" Then Odysseus
spoke—he was standing near me—"Yes, and rightly,"
he said, "they gave them, boy. For it was I
who rescued them and him, their former owner."
My anger got the better of me; I cursed him outright
with every insult that I knew, sparing none,
if he should take my arms away from me.
He is no way given to quarreling, but at this
he was stung by what I said. He answered:
"You were not where we were. You were at home,
out of the reach of duty. Since, besides,
you have so bold a tongue in your head, never   380
will you possess them to bring home to Scyrus."

There it was, abuse on both sides. But I lost
what should be mine and so sailed home. Odysseus,
that filthy son of filthy parents, robbed me.
Yet I do not blame him even so much as the princes.
All of a city is in the hand of the prince,
all of an army; unruly men become so
by the instruction of their betters.
This is the whole tale. May he that hates the Atridae
be as dear in the Gods' sight as he is in mine.   390

Chorus

Earth, Mountain Mother, in whom we find sustenance,
Mother of Zeus himself,
Dweller in great golden Pactolus,
Mother that I dread:
on that other day, too, I called on thee, Thou Blessed One,
Thou that rides on the Bull-killing Lions,
when all the insolence of the Atridae assaulted our Prince,
when they gave his arms, that wonder of the world,   400
    to the son of Laertes.

Philoctetes

You have sailed here, as it seems, with a clear tally;
your half of sorrow matches that of mine.
What you tell me rings in harmony. I recognize
the doings of the Atridae and Odysseus.
I know Odysseus would employ his tongue
on every ill tale, every rascality,
that could be brought to issue in injustice.
This is not at all my wonder, but that Ajax   410
the Elder should stand by, see and allow it.

Neoptolemus

He is no longer living, sir; never, indeed,
if he were, would they have robbed me of the arms.

Philoctetes

What! Is he, too, dead and gone?

Neoptolemus

Yes, dead and gone. As such now think of him.

Philoctetes

But not the son of Tydeus nor Odysseus
whom Sisyphus once sold to Laertes,
they will not die; for they should not be living.

Neoptolemus

Of course, they are not dead; you may be sure
that they are in their glory among the Greeks.   420

Philoctetes

What of an old and honest man, my friend,
Nestor of Pylos? Is he alive? He used
to check their mischief by his wise advice.

Neoptolemus

Things have gone badly for him. He has lost
his son Antilochus, who once stood by him.

Philoctetes

Ah!
You have told me the two deaths that most could hurt me.
Alas, what should I look for
when Ajax and Antilochus are dead,
and still Odysseus lives, that in their stead
ought to be counted among the dead?   430

Neoptolemus

A cunning wrestler; still, Philoctetes,
even the cunning are sometimes tripped up.

Philoctetes

Tell me, by the Gods, where was Patroclus,
who was your father's dearest friend?

Neoptolemus

Dead, too.
In one short sentence I can tell you this.
War never takes a bad man but by chance,
the good man always.

Philoctetes

You have said the truth.
So I will ask you of one quite unworthy
but dexterous and clever with his tongue.   440

Neoptolemus

Whom can you mean except Odysseus?

Philoctetes

It is not he: there was a man, Thersites,
who never was content to speak once only,
though no one was for letting him speak at all.
Do you know if he is still alive?

Neoptolemus

I did not know him,
but I have heard that he is still alive.

Philoctetes

He would be; nothing evil has yet perished.
The Gods somehow give them most excellent care.
They find their pleasure in turning back from Death
the rogues and tricksters, but the just and good
they are always sending out of the world.   450
How can I reckon the score, how can I praise,
when praising Heaven I find the Gods are bad?

Neoptolemus

For my own part, Philoctetes of Oeta,
from now on I shall take precautions.
I shall look at Troy and the Atridae both
from very far off. I shall never abide
the company of those where the worse man
has more power than the better, where the good
are always on the wane and cowards rule.
For the future, rocky Scyrus will content me
to take my pleasure at home.   460
Now I will be going to my ship. Philoctetes,
on you God's blessing and goodbye. May the Gods

recover you of your sickness, as you would have it!
Let us go, men, that when God grants us sailing
we may be ready to sail.

Philoctetes

                  Boy, are you going,
going now?

Neoptolemus

           Yes, the weather favors.
We must look to sail almost at once.

Philoctetes

My dear—I beg you in your father's name,
and in your mother's, in the name of all
that you have loved at home, do not leave me here   470
alone, living in sufferings you have seen
and others I have told you of.
I am not your main concern; give me a passing thought.
I know that there is horrible discomfort
in having me on board. Put up with it.
To such as you and your nobility,
meanness is shameful, decency honorable.
If you leave me here, it is an ugly story.
If you take me, men will say their best of you,
if I shall live to see Oetean land.
Come! One day, hardly one whole day's space   480
that I shall trouble you. Endure this much.
Take me and put me where you will,
in the hold, in the prow or poop, anywhere
where I shall least offend those that I sail with.
By Zeus himself, God of the Suppliants,
I beg you, boy, say "Yes," say you will do it.
Here I am on my knees to you, poor cripple,
for all my lameness. Do not cast me away
so utterly alone, where no one even walks by.
Either take me and set me safe in your own home,
or take me to Chalcedon in Euboea.

From there it will be no great journey for me   490
to Oeta or to ridgy Trachis or
to quick-flowing Spercheius,
and so you show me to my loving father.
For many a day I have feared that he is dead.
With those who came to my island I sent messages,
and many of them, begging him to come
and bring me home himself. Either he's dead,
or, as I rather think, my messengers
made little of what I asked them and hurried home.
Now in you I have found both escort and messenger;   500
bring me safe home. Take pity on me.
Look how men live, always precariously
balanced between good and bad fortune.
If you are out of trouble, watch for danger.
And when you live well, then consider the most
your life, lest ruin take it unawares.

Chorus

Have pity on him, prince.
He has has told us of a most desperate course run.
God forbid such things should overtake friends of mine.
And, prince, if you hate the abdominable Atridae   510
I would set their ill treatment of him
to his gain and would carry him
in your quick, well-fitted ship
to his home and so avoid offense before the face of God.

Neoptolemus

Take care that your assent is not too ready,
and that, when you have enough of his diseased company,   520
you are no longer constant to what you have said.

Chorus

No. You will never be able in this
to reproach me with justice.

Neoptolemus

               I should be ashamed
to be less ready than you to render a stranger service.
Well, if you will then, let us sail. Let him
get ready quickly. My ship will carry him.

May God give us a safe clearance from this land
and a safe journey where we choose to go.

Philoctetes

  God bless this day!   530
  Man, dear to my very heart,
  and you, dear friends, how shall I prove to you
  how you have bound me to your friendship!
  Let us go, boy. But let us first kiss the earth,
  reverently, in my homeless home of a cave.
  I would have you know what I have lived from,
  how tough the spirit that did not break. I think
  the sight itself would have been enough for anyone
  except myself. Necessity has taught me,
  little by little, to suffer and be patient.

Chorus

  Wait! Let us see. Two men are coming.
  One of them is of our crew, the other a foreigner.   540
  Let us hear from them and then go in.

                 (Enter the Sailor disguised as a Trader.)

Trader

  Son of Achilles, I told my fellow traveler here—
  he with two others were guarding your ship—
  to tell me where you were. I happened on you.
  I had no intentions this way. Just by accident
  I came to anchor at this island.
  I am sailing in command of a ship outward bound
  from Ilium, with no great company, for Peparethus—
  a good country, that, for wine. When I heard
  that all those sailors were the crew of your ship,   550

I thought I should not hold my tongue and sail on
until I spoke with you—and got my reward,
a fair one, doubtless. Apparently you do not know
much of your own affairs, nor what new plans
the Greeks have for you. Indeed, not only plans,
actions in train already and not slowly.

Neoptolemus

Thank you for your consideration, sir.
I will remain obliged to your kindness
unless I prove unworthy. Please tell me
what you have spoken of. I would like to know
what are these new plans of the Greeks. 560

Trader

Old Phoenix and the two sons of Theseus are gone,
pursuing you with a squadron.

Neoptolemus

Do they intend
to bring me back with violence or persuade me?

Trader

I do not know. I tell you what I heard.

Neoptolemus

Are Phoenix and his friends in such a hurry
to do the bidding of the two Atridae?

Trader

It is being done.
There is no delay about it. That you should know.

Neoptolemus

How is it that Odysseus was not ready
to sail as his own messenger on such
an errand? It cannot be he was afraid?

Trader

When I weighed anchor, he and Tydeus' son 570
were in pursuit of still another man.

Neoptolemus

Who was this other man that Odysseus himself should seek him?

Trader

There was a man—perhaps you will tell me first
who this is; and say softly what you say.

Neoptolemus

This, sir, is the famous Philoctetes.

Trader

Do not
ask me any further questions. Get yourself out,
as quickly as you can, out of this island.

Philoctetes

What does he say, boy? Why in dark whispers
does he bargain with you about me, this sailor?

Neoptolemus

I do not know yet what he says, but he must say it,
openly, whatever it is, to you and me and these.

580

Trader

Son of Achilles, do not slander me,
speaking of me to the army as a tattler.
There's many a thing I do for them and in return
get something from them, as a poor man may.

Neoptolemus

I am the enemy of the Atridae. This
is my greatest friend because he hates the Atridae.
You have come to me as a friend, and so you must
hide from me nothing that you heard.

Trader

Well, watch what you are doing, sir.

Neoptolemus

I have.

Trader

I put the whole responsibility
squarely upon yourself.

Neoptolemus

Do so; but speak.

590

Trader

Well, then. The two I have spoken of,
the son of Tydeus and the Prince Odysseus,
are in pursuit of Philoctetes.
They have sworn, so help them God, to bring him with them
either by persuasion or by brute force.
And this all the Greeks heard clearly announced
by Prince Odysseus; for he was much surer
of success than was the other.

Neoptolemus

What can have made

the Atridae care about him after so long—
one whom they, years and years since, cast away?
What yearning for him came over them? Was it the Gods
who punish evil doings that now have driven them
to retribution for injustice?

600

Trader

I will explain all that. Perhaps you haven't heard.
There was a prophet of very good family,
a son of Priam indeed, called Helenus.
He was captured one night in an expedition
undertaken singlehanded by Odysseus,
of whom all base and shameful things are spoken,
captured by stratagem. Odysseus brought
his prisoner before the Greeks, a splendid prize.
Helenus prophesied everything to them
and, in particular, touching the fortress of Troy,
that they could never take it till they persuaded
Philoctetes to come with them and leave his island.
As soon as Odysseus heard the prophet say this,
he promised at once to bring the man before them,
for all to see—he thought, as a willing prisoner,
but, if not that, against his will. If he failed,

610

"any of them might have his head," he declared. My boy,
that is the whole story; that is why I urge you   620
and him and any that you care for to make haste.

Philoctetes

Ah!
Did he indeed swear that he would persuade me
to sail with him, did he so, that utter devil?
As soon shall I be persuaded, when I am dead,
to rise from Death's house, come to the light again,
as his own father did.

Trader

I do not know about that. Well, I will be going now
to my ship. May God prosper you both!

(*Exit Trader.*)

Philoctetes

Is it not terrible, boy, that this Odysseus
should think that there are words soft enough to win me,
to let him put me in his boat, exhibit me
in front of all the Greeks?   630
No! I would rather listen to my worst enemy,
the snake that bit me, made me into this cripple.
But he can say anything, he can dare anything.
Now I know that he will come here.
Boy, let us go, that a great sea may sever
us from Odysseus' ship.
Let us go. For look, haste in due season shown
brings rest and peace when once the work is done.

Neoptolemus

When the wind at our prow falls, we can sail, no sooner.
Now it is dead against us.   640

Philoctetes

It is always fair sailing, when you escape evil.

Neoptolemus

Yes, but the wind is against them, too.

Philoctetes
> For pirates
when they can thieve and plunder, no wind is contrary.

Neoptolemus
> If you will, then, let us go. Take from your cave
> what you need most and love most.

Philoctetes
> There are some things I need, but no great choice.

Neoptolemus
> What is there that you will not find on board?

Philoctetes
> A herb I have, the chief means to soothe my wound,
> to lull the pain to sleep.   650

Neoptolemus
> Bring it out then.
> What else is there that you would have?

Philoctetes
> Any arrow
> I may have dropped and missed. For none of them
> must I leave for another to pick up.

Neoptolemus
> Is this, in your hands, the famous bow?

Philoctetes
> Yes, this,
> this in my hands.

Neoptolemus
> May I see it closer,
> touch and adore it like a god?

Philoctetes
> You may have it
> and anything else of mine that is for your good.

Neoptolemus
> I long for it, yet only with such longing   660

that if it is lawful, I may have it, else
let it be.

Philoctetes

      Your words are holy, boy. It is lawful.
for you have given me, and you alone,
the sight of the sun shining above us here,
the sight of my Oeta, of my old father, my friends.
You have raised me up above my enemies,
when I was under their feet. You may be confident.
You may indeed touch my bow, give it again
to me that gave it you, proclaim that alone
of all the world you touched it, in return
for the good deed you did. It was for that,
for friendly help, I myself won it first.   670

Neoptolemus

I am glad to see you and take you as a friend.
For one who knows how to show and to accept kindness
will be a friend better than any possession.
Go in.

Philoctetes

     I will bring you with me. The sickness in me
seeks to have you beside me.

Chorus

In story I have heard, but my eyes have not seen
him that once would have drawn near to Zeus's bed.
I have heard how he caught him, bound him on a running wheel,
Zeus, son of Kronos, invincible.
But I know of no other,   680
by hearsay, much less by sight, of all mankind
whose destiny was more his enemy when he met it
than Philoctetes', who wronged no one, nor killed
but lived, just among the just,
and fell in trouble past his deserts.
There is wonder, indeed, in my heart
how, how in his loneliness,

listening to the waves beating on the shore,
how he kept hold at all
on a life so full of tears.   690

He was lame, and no one came near him.
He suffered, and there were no neighbors for his sorrow
with whom his cries would find answer,
with whom he could lament the bloody plague
that ate him up.
No one who would gather
fallen leaves from the ground
to quiet the raging, bleeding sore,
running, in his maggot-rotten foot.   700
Here and there he crawled
writhing always—
suffering like a child
without the nurse he loves—
to what source of ease he could find
when the heart-devouring suffering gave over.

No grain sown in holy earth was his, nor other food
of all enjoyed by us, men who live by labor,
save when with the feathered arrows shot by the quick bow   710
he got him fodder for his belly.
Alas, poor soul,
that never in ten years' length
enjoyed a drink of wine
but looked always for the standing pools
and approached them.
But now he will end fortunate. He has fallen in
with the son of good men. He will be great, after it all.   720
Our prince in his seaworthy craft will carry him
after the fulness of many months, to his father's home
in the country of the Malian nymphs,
by the banks of the Spercheius,

where the hero of the bronze shield ascended
to all the Gods, ablaze in holy fire
above the ridges of Oeta.

Neoptolemus

Come if you will, then. Why have you nothing to say?   730
Why do you stand, in silence transfixed?

Philoctetes

Oh! Oh!

Neoptolemus

What is it?

Philoctetes

Nothing to be afraid of. Come on, boy.

Neoptolemus

Is it the pain of your inveterate sickness?

Philoctetes

No, no, indeed not. Just now I think I feel better.
O Gods!

Neoptolemus

Why do you call on the Gods with cries of distress?

Philoctetes

That they may come as healers, come with gentleness.
Oh! Oh!

Neoptolemus

What ails you? Tell me; do not keep silence.   740
You are clearly in some pain.

Philoctetes

I am lost, boy.
I will not be able to hide it from you longer.
Oh! Oh!
It goes through me, right through me!
Miserable, miserable!
I am lost, boy. I am being eaten up. Oh!

By God, if you have a sword, ready to hand, use it!
Strike the end of my foot. Strike it off, I tell you, now.
Do not spare my life. Quick, boy, quick.   750

(A long silence.)

Neoptolemus
What is this thing that comes upon you suddenly,
that makes you cry and moan so?

Philoctetes
                              Do you know, boy?

Neoptolemus
What is it?

Philoctetes
              Do you know, boy?

Neoptolemus
                              What do you mean?
I do not know.

Philoctetes
                  Surely you know. Oh! Oh!

Neoptolemus
The terrible burden of your sickness.

Philoctetes
Terrible it is, beyond words' reach. But pity me.

Neoptolemus
What shall I do?

Philoctetes
                  Do not be afraid and leave me.
She comes from time to time, perhaps when she has had
her fill of wandering in other places.

Neoptolemus
You most unhappy man,
you that have endured all agonies, lived through them,   760
shall I take hold of you? Shall I touch you?

Philoctetes

Not that, above everything. But take this bow,
as you asked to do just now, until the pain,
the pain of my sickness, that is now upon me, grows less.
Keep the bow, guard it safely. Sleep comes upon me
when the attack is waning. The pain will not end till then.
But you must let me sleep quietly.
If they should come in the time when I sleep,
by the Gods I beg you do not give up my bow   770
willingly or unwillingly to anyone.
And let no one trick you out of it, lest you prove
a murderer—your own and mine that kneeled to you.

Neoptolemus

I shall take care; be easy about that. It shall not pass
except to your hands and to mine. Give it to me now,
and may good luck go with it!

Philoctetes

                        Here,
take it, boy. Bow in prayer to the Gods' envy
that the bow may not be to you a sorrow
nor as it was to me and its former master.

Neoptolemus

You Gods, grant us both this and grant us
a journey speedy with a prosperous wind   780
to where God sends us and our voyage holds.

Philoctetes

An empty prayer, I am afraid, boy:
the blood is trickling, dripping murderously
from its deep spring. I look for something new.
It is coming now, coming. Ah!
You have the bow. Do not go away from me.
        Ah!
O man of Cephallenia, would it were you,
Would it were your breast that the pains transfix.
        Ah!   790

Agamemnon and Menelaus, my two generals,
would it were your two bodies that had fed
this sickness for as long as mine has. Ah!

Death, death, how is it that I can call on you,
always, day in, day out, and you cannot come to me?
Boy, my good boy, take up this body of mine
and burn it on what they call the Lemnian fire.   800
I had the resolution once to do this for another,
the son of Zeus, and so obtained the arms
that you now hold. What do you say?
What do you say? Nothing? Where are you, boy?

Neoptolemus
I have been in pain for you; I have been
in sorrow for your pain.

Philoctetes
No, boy, keep up your heart. She is quick in coming
and quick to go. Only I entreat you, do not
leave me alone.

Neoptolemus
Do not be afraid. We shall stay.   810

Philoctetes
You will?

Neoptolemus
You may be sure of it.

Philoctetes
Your oath,
I do not think it fit to put you to your oath.

Neoptolemus
I *may* not go without you, Philoctetes.

Philoctetes
Give me your hand upon it.

Neoptolemus
    Here I give it you,
    to remain.

Philoctetes
    Now—take me away from here—

Neoptolemus
                            What do you mean?

Philoctetes
                                            Up, up.

Neoptolemus
    What madness is upon you? Why do you look
    on the sky above us?

Philoctetes
                    Let me go, let me go.

Neoptolemus
    Where?

Philoctetes
            Oh, let me go.

Neoptolemus
                    Not I.

Philoctetes
    You will kill me if you touch me.

Neoptolemus
    Now I shall let you go, now you are calmer.

Philoctetes
    Earth, take my body, dying as I am.
    The pain no longer lets me stand.   820

Neoptolemus
    In a little while, I think,
    sleep will come on this man. His head is nodding.
    The sweat is soaking all his body over,
    and a black flux of blood and matter has broken
    out of his foot. Let us leave him quiet, friends,
    until he falls asleep.

Chorus

Sleep that knows not pain nor suffering
kindly upon us, Lord,
kindly, kindly come.
Spread your enveloping radiance,   830
as now, over his eyes.
Come, come, Lord Healer.

Boy, look to your standing,
look to your going, look to your plans
for the future. Do you see? He sleeps.
What is it we are waiting to do?
Ripeness that holds decision over all things
wins many a victory suddenly.

Neoptolemus

Yes, it is true he hears nothing, but I see we have hunted in vain,
vainly have captured our quarry the bow, if we sail without him.   840
His is the crown of victory, him the God said we must bring.
Shame shall be ours if we boast and our lies still leave victory
    unwon.

Chorus

Boy, to all of this the God shall look.
Answer me gently;
low, low, whisper,
whisper, boy.
The sleep of a sick man has keen eyes.
It is a sleep unsleeping.

But to the limits of what you can,
look to this, look to this secretly,   850
how you may do it.
You know of whom I speak.
If your mind holds the same purpose touching this man,
the wise can see trouble and no way to cure it.
It is a fair wind, boy, a fair wind:
the man is eyeless and helpless,

outstretched under night's blanket—
asleep in the sun is good—
neither of foot nor of hand nor of anything is he master,   860
but is even as one that lies in Death's house.
Look to it, look if what you say
is seasonable. As far as my mind,
boy, can grasp it, best is the trouble taken
that causes the least fear.

Neoptolemus

Quiet, I tell you! Are you mad? He is stirring,
his eyes are stirring; he is raising his head.

Philoctetes

Blessed the light that comes after my sleep,
blessed the watching of friends.
I never would have hoped this,
that you would have the pity of heart to support   870
my afflictions, that you should stand by me and help.
The Atridae, those brave generals, were not so,
they could not so easily put up with me.
You have a noble nature, Neoptolemus,
and noble were your parents. You have made light
of all of this—the offense of my cries and the smell.
And now, since it would seem I can forget
my sickness for a while and rest, raise me yourself,
raise me up, boy, and set me on my feet,
that when my weariness releases me,
we can go to the ship and sail without delay.   880

Neoptolemus

I am glad to see you unexpectedly,
eyes open, free of pain, still with the breath of life.
With suffering like yours, all the signs pointed
to your being dead. Now, lift yourself up.
If you would rather, these men will lift you. They
will spare no trouble, since you and I are agreed.

Philoctetes

 Thanks, boy. Lift me yourself, as you thought of it.
 Do not trouble them, let them not be disquieted   890
 before they need by the foul smell of me; living
 on board with me will try their patience enough.

Neoptolemus

 Very well, then; stand on your feet; take hold yourself.

Philoctetes

 Do not be afraid; old habit will help me up.

Neoptolemus

 Now is the moment. What shall I do from now on?

Philoctetes

 What is it, boy? Where are your words straying?

Neoptolemus

 I do not know what to say. I am at a loss.

Philoctetes

 Why are you at a loss? Do not say so, boy.

Neoptolemus

 It is indeed my case.

Philoctetes

 Is it disgust at my sickness? Is it this   900
 that makes you shrink from taking me?

Neoptolemus

 All is disgust when one leaves his own nature
 and does things that misfit it.

Philoctetes

 It is not unlike your father, either in word
 or in act, to help a good man.

Neoptolemus

 I shall be shown to be dishonorable:
 I am afraid of that.

Philoctetes

Not in your present actions. Your words make me hesitate.

Neoptolemus

Zeus, what must I do? Twice be proved base,
hiding what I should not, saying what is most foul?

Philoctetes

Unless I am wrong, here is a man who will   910
betray me, leave me—so it seems—and sail away.

Neoptolemus

Not I; I will not leave you. To your bitterness,
I shall send you on a journey—and I dread this.

Philoctetes

What are you saying, boy? I do not understand.

Neoptolemus

I will not hide anything. You must sail to Troy
to the Achaeans, join the army of the Atridae.

Philoctetes

What! What can you mean?

Neoptolemus

                          Do not cry yet
until you learn.

Philoctetes

Learn what? What would you do with me?

Neoptolemus

First save you from this torture, then with you
go and lay waste the land of Troy.   920

Philoctetes

                          You would?
This is, in truth, what you intend?

Neoptolemus

                          Necessity,
a great necessity compels it. Do not be angry.

Philoctetes

    Then I am lost. I am betrayed. Why, stranger,
    have you done this to me? Give me back my bow.

Neoptolemus

    That I cannot. Justice and interest
    make me obedient to those in authority.

Philoctetes

    You fire, you every horror, most hateful engine
    of ruthless mischief, what have you done to me,
    what treachery! Have you no shame to see me
    that kneeled to you, entreated you, hard of heart?   930

    You robbed me of my livelihood, taking my bow.
    Give it back, I beg you, give it back, I pray, my boy!
    By your father's Gods, do not take my livelihood.
    He does not say a word,
    but turns away his eyes. He will not give it up.

    Caverns and headlands, dens of wild creatures,
    you jutting broken crags, to you I raise my cry—
    there is no one else that I can speak to—
    and you have always been there, have always heard me,
    Let me tell you what he has done to me, this boy,   940
    Achilles' son. He swore to bring me home;
    he brings me to Troy. He gave me his right hand,
    then took and keeps my sacred bow,
    the bow of Heracles, the son of Zeus,
    and means to show it to the Argives,
    as though in me he had conquered a strong man,
    as though he led me captive to his power.
    He does not know he is killing one that is dead,
    a kind of vaporous shadow, a mere wraith.
    Had I had my strength, he had not conquered me,
    for, even as I am, it was craft that did it.
    I have been deceived and am lost.
    What can I do?

Give it back. Be your true self again. Will you not? 950
No word. Then I am nothing.

Two doors cut in the rock, to you again,
again I come, enter again, unarmed,
no means to feed myself! Here in this passage
I shall shrivel to death alone. I shall kill no more,
neither winged bird nor wild thing of the hills
with this my bow. I shall myself in death
be a feast for those that fed me. Those that I hunted
shall be my hunters now.
Life for the life I took, I shall repay
at the hands of this man that seemed to know no harm. 960

My curse upon your life!—but not yet still
until I know if you will change again;
if you will not, may an evil death be yours!

Chorus

What shall we do? Shall we sail? Shall we do as he asks?
Prince, it is you must decide.

Neoptolemus

A kind of compassion,
a terrible compassion, has come upon me
for him. I have felt for him all the time.

Philoctetes

Pity me, boy, by the Gods; do not bring on yourself
men's blame for your crafty victory over me.

Neoptolemus

What shall I do? I would I had never left
Scyrus, so hateful is what I face now. 970

Philoctetes

You are not bad yourself; by bad men's teaching
you came to practice your foul lesson. Leave it to others
such as it suits, and sail away. Give me my arms.

Neoptolemus
What shall we do, men?

(*Odysseus appears.*)

Odysseus
Scoundrel, what are you doing? Give me those arms.

Philoctetes
Who is this? Is that Odysseus' voice?

Odysseus
It is.
Odysseus certainly; you can see him here.

Philoctetes
Then I have been sold indeed; I am lost. It was he
who took me prisoner, robbed me of my arms.

Odysseus
Yes, I, I and no other. I admit that.   980

Philoctetes
Boy, give me back my bow, give it back to me.

Odysseus
That he will never
be able to do now, even if he wishes it.
And you must come with the bow, or these will
bring you.

Philoctetes
Your wickedness and impudence are without limit.
Will these men bring me, then, against my will?

Odysseus
Yes, if you do not come with a good grace.

Philoctetes
O land of Lemnos and all mastering brightness,
Hephaestus-fashioned, must I indeed bear this,
that he, Odysseus, drags me from you with violence?

Odysseus
It is Zeus, I would have you know, Zeus this land's ruler,
who has determined. I am only his servant.   990

Philoctetes

> Hateful creature,
> what things you can invent! You plead the Gods
> to screen your actions and make the Gods out liars.

Odysseus

> They speak the truth. The road must be traveled.

Philoctetes

> I say No.

Odysseus

> I say Yes. You must listen.

Philoctetes

> Are we slaves and not free? Is it as such
> our fathers have begotten us?

Odysseus

> No, but as equals
> of the best, with whom it is destined you must take Troy,
> dig her down stone by stone.

Philoctetes

> Never, I would rather suffer anything than this.
> There is still my steep and rugged precipice here.   1000

Odysseus

> What do you mean to do?

Philoctetes

> Throw myself down,
> shatter my head upon the rock below.

Odysseus

> Hold him. Take this solution out of his power.

Philoctetes

> Hands of mine, quarry of Odysseus' hunting,
> now suffer in your lack of the loved bowstring!
>
> You who have never had a healthy thought
> nor noble, you Odysseus, how you have hunted me,
> how you have stolen upon me with this boy

as your shield, because I did not know him, one
that is no mate for you but worthy of me,
who knows nothing but to do what he was bidden,   1010
and now, you see, is suffering bitterly
for his own faults and what he brought on me.
Your shabby, slit-eyed soul taught him step by step
to be clever in mischief against his nature and will.
Now it is my turn, now to my sorrow you have me
bound hand and foot, intend to take me away,
away from this shore on which you cast me once
without friends or comrades or city, a dead man among the living.

My curse on you! I have often cursed you before,
but the Gods give me nothing that is sweet to me.   1020
You have joy to be alive, and I have sorrow
because my very life is linked to this pain,
laughed at by you and your two generals,
the sons of Atreus whom you serve in this.
And yet, when you sailed with them, it was by constraint
and trickery, while I came of my own free will
with seven ships, to my undoing, I
whom they dishonored and cast away—
you say it was they that did it and they you.

But now why are you taking me? For what?
I am nothing now. To you all I have long been dead.   1030
God-hated wretch, how is it that now I am not
lame and foul-smelling? How can you burn your sacrifice
to God if I sail with you? Pour your libations?
This was your excuse for casting me away.

May death in ugly form come on you! It will so come,
for you have wronged me, if the Gods care for justice.
And I know that they do care for it, for at present
you never would have sailed here for my sake
and my happiness, had not the goad of God,

a need of me, compelled you.
Land of my fathers, Gods that look on men's deeds,   1040
take vengeance on these men, in your own good time,
upon them all, if you have pity on me!
Wretchedly as I live, if I saw them
dead, I could dream that I was free of my sickness.

Chorus

He is a hard man, Odysseus, this stranger,
and hard his words: no yielding to suffering in them.

Odysseus

If I had the time, I have much I could say to him.
As it is, there is only one thing. As the occasion
demands, such a one am I.
When there is a competition of men just and good,   1050
you will find none more scrupulous than myself.
What I seek in everything is to win
except in your regard: I willingly yield to you now.

Let him go, men. Do not lay a finger on him.
Let him stay here. We have these arms of yours
and do not need you, Philoctetes.
Teucer is with us who has the skill and I,
who, I think, am no meaner master of them
and have as straight an aim. Why do we need you?
Farewell: pace Lemnos. Let us go. Perhaps   1060
your prize will bring me the honor you should have had.

Philoctetes

What shall I do? Will you appear
before the Argives in the glory of my arms?

Odysseus

Say nothing further to me. I am going.

Philoctetes

Your voice has no word for me, son of Achilles?
Will you go away in silence?

Odysseus

Come, Neoptolemus.
Do not look at him. Your generosity
may spoil our future.

Philoctetes

You, too, men, will you go   1070
and leave me alone? Do you, too, have no pity?

Chorus

This young man is our captain. What he says to you
we say as well.

Neoptolemus (to the Chorus)

Odysseus will tell me
that I am full of pity for him. Still
remain, if he will have it so, as long
as it takes the sailors to ready the tackle
and until we have made our prayer to the Gods.
Perhaps, in the meantime, he will have better thoughts
about us. Let us go, Odysseus.
You, when we call you, be quick to come.   1080

(Exeunt Odysseus and Neoptolemus.)

Philoctetes

Hollow in the rock, hollow cave, sun-warmed, ice cold,
I was not destined, after all, ever to leave you.
Still with me, you shall be witness to my dying.
Passageway, crowded with my cries of pain,
what shall be, now again, my daily life with you?
What hope shall I find of food to keep my wretched life alive?   1090
Above me, in the clouds, down the shrill winds
the birds; no strength in me to stop them.

Chorus

It was you who doomed yourself,
man of hard fortune. From no other,
from nothing stronger, came your mischance.
When you could have chosen wisdom,

with better opportunity before you,
you chose the worse.   1100

Philoctetes

Sorrow, sorrow is mine. Suffering has broken me,
who must live henceforth alone from all the world,
must live here and die here;
no longer bringing home food nor winning
it with strong hands. Unmarked, the crafty words   1110
of a treacherous heart stole on me. Would I might see him,
contriver of this trap,
for as long as I am, condemned to pain.

Chorus

It was the will of the Gods
that has subdued you, no craft
to which my hand was lent.   1120
Turn your hate, your ill-omened curses, elsewhere.
This indeed lies near my heart,
that you should not reject my friendship.

Philoctetes

By the shore of the gray sea he sits and laughs at me.
He brandishes in his hand the weapon which kept me alive,
which no one else had handled. Bow that I loved,
forged from the hands that loved you, if you could feel,
you would see me with pity, successor to Heracles,   1130
that used you and shall handle you no more.
You have found a new master, a man of craft, and shall be bent
   by him.
You shall see crooked deceits and the face of my hateful foe,
and a thousand ill things such as he contrived against me.

Chorus

A man should give careful heed to say what is just;   1140
and when he has said it, restrain his tongue from rancor and taunt.
Odysseus was one man, appointed by many,
by their command he has done this, a service to his friends.

Philoctetes

    Birds my victims, tribes of bright-eyed wild creatures,
    tenants of these hills, you need not flee from me or my house.
    No more the strength of my hands, of my bow, is mine.   1150
    Come! It is a good time
    to glut yourselves freely on my discolored flesh.
    For shortly I shall die here. How shall I find means of life?
    Who can live on air without any of all that life-giving earth sup-
        plies?   1160

Chorus

    In the name of the gods, if there is anything that you hold in re-
        spect,
    draw near to a friend that approaches you in all sincerity.
    Know what you are doing, know it well.
    It lies with you to avoid your doom.
    It is a destiny pitiable to feed
    with your body. It cannot learn how
    to endure the thousand burdens with which it is coupled.

Philoctetes

    Again, again you have touched my old hurt,   1170
    for all that you are the best of those that came here.
    Why did you afflict me? What have you done to me?

Chorus

    What do you mean by this?

Philoctetes

    Yes, you have hoped to bring me
    to the hateful land of Troy.

Chorus

    I judge that to be best.

Philoctetes

    Then leave me now at once.

Chorus

    Glad news, glad news.
    I am right willing to obey you.
    Let us go now to our places in the ship.   1180

Philoctetes

No, by the God that listens to curses, do not go,
I beseech you.

Chorus

Be calm!

Philoctetes

Friends, stay!
I beg you to stay.

Chorus

Why do you call on us?

Philoctetes

It is the God, the God. I am destroyed.
My foot, what shall I do with this foot of mine
in the life I shall live hereafter?
Friends, come to me again.   1190

Chorus

What to do that is different
from the tenor of your former bidding?

Philoctetes

It is no occasion for anger
when a man crazy with storms of sorrow
speaks against his better judgment.

Chorus

Unhappy man, come with us, as we say.

Philoctetes

Never, never! That is my fixed purpose.
Not though the Lord of the Lightning, bearing his fiery bolts,
come against me, burning me
with flame and glare.
Let Ilium go down and all that under its walls   1200
had the heart to cast me away, crippled!
Friends, grant me one prayer only.

Chorus

What is it you would seek?

Philoctetes

    A sword, if you have got one,
    or an ax or some weapon—give it me!

Chorus

    What would you do with it?

Philoctetes

                   Head and foot,
    head and foot, all of me, I would cut with my own hand.
    My mind is set on death, on death, I tell you.

Chorus

    Why this?   1210

Philoctetes

            I would go seek my father.

Chorus

    Where?

Philoctetes

          In the house of death.
    He is no longer in the light.
    City of my fathers, would I could see you.
    I who left your holy streams,
    to go help the Greeks, my enemies,
    and now am nothing any more.

Chorus

    I should have been by now on my way to the ship,
    did I not see Odysseus coming here   1220
    and with him Neoptolemus.

        (*Enter Odysseus and Neoptolemus in front of the cave, talking.*
                          Philoctetes withdraws into the cave.)

Odysseus (to Neoptolemus)

    You have turned back, there is hurry in your step.
    Will you not tell me why?

Neoptolemus

    I go to undo the wrong that I have done.

Odysseus

A strange thing to say! What wrong was that?

Neoptolemus

I did wrong when I obeyed you and the Greeks.

Odysseus

What did we make you do that was unworthy?

Neoptolemus

I practiced craft and treachery with success.

Odysseus

On whom? Would you do some rash thing now?

Neoptolemus

Nothing rash. I am going to give something back.   1230

Odysseus

What? I am afraid to hear what you will say.

Neoptolemus

Back to the man I took it from, this bow.

Odysseus

You cannot mean you are going to give it back.

Neoptolemus

Just that. To my shame, unjustly, I obtained it.

Odysseus

Can you mean this in earnest?

Neoptolemus

                              Yes, unless
it is not in earnest to tell you the truth.

Odysseus

What do you mean, Neoptolemus, what are you saying?

Neoptolemus

Must I tell you the same story twice or thrice?

Odysseus

I should prefer not to have heard it once.

Neoptolemus
You can rest easy. You have now heard everything.   1240

Odysseus
Then there is someone who will prevent its execution.

Neoptolemus
Who will that be?

Odysseus
The whole assembly
of the Greeks and among them I myself.

Neoptolemus
You are a clever man, Odysseus, but
this is not a clever saying.

Odysseus
                    In your own case
neither the words nor the acts are clever.

Neoptolemus
                                        Still
if they are just, they are better than clever.

Odysseus
How can it be just to give to him again
what you won by my plans?

Neoptolemus
It was a sin,
a shameful sin, which I shall try to retrieve.

Odysseus
Have you no fear of the Greeks if you do this?   1250

Neoptolemus
I have no fear of anything you can do,
when I act with justice; nor shall I yield to force.

Odysseus
Then we shall fight
not with the Trojans but with you.

Neoptolemus
Let that be as it will.

Odysseus
           Do you see my hand,
reaching for the sword?

Neoptolemus
             You shall see me do as much
and that at once.

Odysseus
          I will let you alone;
I shall go and tell this to the assembled Greeks,
and they will punish you.

Neoptolemus
            That is very prudent.
If you are always as prudent as this,
perhaps you will keep out of trouble.   1260

                  (*Exit Odysseus.*)

I call on you, Philoctetes, son of Poias,
come from your cave.

      (*Philoctetes appears at the mouth of the cave.*)
Philoctetes
          What cry is this at the door?
Why do you call me forth, friends? What would you have?
Ah! This is a bad thing. Can there be some fresh mischief
you come to do, to top what you have done?

Neoptolemus
Be easy. I would only have you listen.

Philoctetes
I am afraid of that.
I heard you before, and they were good words, too.
But they destroyed me when I listened.

Neoptolemus
Is there no place, then, for repentance?   1270

Philoctetes

    You were just such a one in words when you stole my bow,
    inspiring confidence, but sly and treacherous.

Neoptolemus

    I am not such now. But I would hear from you
    whether you are entirely determined
    to remain here, or will you go with us?

Philoctetes

    Oh, stop! You need not say another word.
    All that you say will be wasted.

Neoptolemus

    You are determined?

Philoctetes

                 More than words can declare.

Neoptolemus

    I wish that I could have persuaded you.
    If I cannot speak to some purpose, I have done.

Philoctetes

    You will say it all   1280
    to no purpose, for you will never win my heart
    to friendship with you, who have stolen my life
    by treachery, and then came and preached to me,
    bad son of a noble father. Cursed be you all,
    first the two sons of Atreus, then Odysseus,
    and then yourself!

Neoptolemus

              Do not curse me any more.
    Take your bow. Here I give it to you.

Philoctetes

    What can you mean? Is this another trick?

Neoptolemus

    No. That I swear by the holy majesty
    of Zeus on high!

Philoctetes

> These are good words,
> if only they are honest.   1290

Neoptolemus

> The fact is plain.
> Stretch out your hand; take your own bow again.

> > (*Odysseus appears.*)

Odysseus

> I forbid it, as the Gods are my witnesses,
> in the name of the Atridae and the Greeks.

Philoctetes

> Whose voice is that, boy? Is it Odysseus?

Odysseus

> Himself and near at hand.
> And I shall bring you to the plains of Troy
> in your despite, whether Achilles' son
> will have it so or not.

Philoctetes

> You will rue your word
> if this arrow flies straight.

Neoptolemus

> > No, Philoctetes, no!   1300
> Do not shoot.

Philoctetes

> > Let me go, let go my hand, dear boy.

Neoptolemus

> I will not.

> > (*Exit Odysseus.*)

Philoctetes

> Why did you prevent me killing my enemy,
> with my bow, a man that hates me?

Neoptolemus

> This is not to our glory, neither yours nor mine.

Philoctetes

    Well, know this much, that the princes of the army,
    the lying heralds of the Greeks, are cowards
    when they meet the spear, however keen in words.

Neoptolemus

    Let that be. You have your bow. There is no further cause
    for anger or reproach against me.

Philoctetes

                    None.

    You have shown your nature and true breeding,   1310
    son of Achilles and not Sisyphus.
    Your father, when he still was with the living,
    was the most famous of them, as now he is of the dead.

Neoptolemus

    I am happy to hear you speak well of my father
    and of myself. Now listen to my request.
    The fortunes that the Gods give to us men
    we must bear under necessity.
    But men that cling wilfully to their sufferings
    as you do, no one may forgive nor pity.   1320
    Your anger has made a savage of you. You will not
    accept advice, although the friend advises
    in pure goodheartedness. You loathe him, think
    he is your enemy and hates you.
    Yet I will speak. May Zeus, the God of Oaths,
    be my witness! Mark it, Philoctetes, write it in your mind.
    You are sick and the pain of the sickness is of God's sending
    because you approached the Guardian of Chryse,
    the serpent that with secret watch protects
    her roofless shrine to keep it from violation.
    You will never know relief while the selfsame sun   1330
    rises before you here, sets there again,
    until you come of your own will to Troy,
    and meet among us the Asclepiadae,

who will relieve your sickness; then with the bow
and by my side, you will become Troy's conqueror.

I will tell you how I know that this is so.
There was a man of Troy who was taken prisoner,
Helenus, a good prophet. He told us clearly
how it should be and said, besides, that all Troy   1340
must fall this summer. He said, "If I prove wrong
you may kill me."
Now since you know this, yield and be gracious.
It is a glorious heightening of gain.
First, to come into hands that can heal you,
and then be judged pre-eminent among the Greeks,
winning the highest renown among them, taking
Troy that has cost infinity of tears.

Philoctetes

Hateful life, why should I still be alive and seeing?
Why not be gone to the dark?
What shall I do? How can I distrust   1350
his words who in friendship has counseled me?
Shall I then yield? If I do so, how come
before the eyes of men so miserable?
Who will say word of greeting to me?
Eyes of mine, that have seen all, can you endure
to see me living with my murderers,
the sons of Atreus? With cursed Odysseus?
It is not the sting of wrongs past
but what I must look for in wrongs to come.
Men whose wit has been mother of villainy once   1360
have learned from it to be evil in all things.
I must indeed wonder at yourself in this.
You should not yourself be going to Troy
but rather hold me back. They have done you wrong
and robbed you of your father's arms. Will you go and help them
fight and compel me to the like?
No, boy, no; take me home as you promised.

Remain in Scyrus yourself; let these bad men
die in their own bad fashion. We shall both thank you,   1370
I and your father. You will not then, by helping
the wicked, seem to be like them.

Neoptolemus

What you say
is reasonable; yet I wish that you would trust
the Gods, my word, and, with me as friend, fare forth.

Philoctetes

What, to the plains of Troy, to the cursed sons
of Atreus with this suffering foot of mine?

Neoptolemus

To those that shall give you redress,
that shall save you and your rotting foot from its disease.

Philoctetes

Giver of dread advice, what have you said!   1380

Neoptolemus

What I see fulfilled will be best for you and me.

Philoctetes

And saying it, do you not blush before God?

Neoptolemus

Why should one feel ashamed to do good to another?

Philoctetes

Is the good for the Atridae or for me?

Neoptolemus

I am your friend, and the word I speak is friendly.

Philoctetes

How, then, do you wish to betray me to my enemies?

Neoptolemus

Sir, learn not to be defiant in misfortune.

Philoctetes

You will ruin me, I know it by your words.

Neoptolemus
Not I. You do not understand, I think.

Philoctetes
Do I not know the Atridae cast me away?   1390

Neoptolemus
They cast you away; will, now again, restore you.

Philoctetes
Never, if of my will I must see Troy.

Neoptolemus
What shall we do, since I cannot convince you
of anything I say? It is easiest for me
to leave my argument, and you to live,
as you are living, with no hope of cure.

Philoctetes
Let me suffer what I must suffer.
But what you promised to me and touched my hand,
to bring me home, fulfil it for me, boy.
Do not delay, do not speak again of Troy   1400
I have had enough of sorrow and lamentation.

Neoptolemus
If you will then, let us go.

Philoctetes
Noble is the word you spoke.

Neoptolemus
Brace yourself, stand firm on your feet.

Philoctetes
To the limit of my strength.

Neoptolemus
How shall I avoid the blame of the Greeks?

Philoctetes
Give it no thought.

Neoptolemus

What if they come and harry my country?

Philoctetes

I shall be there.

Neoptolemus

What help will you be able to give me?

Philoctetes

With the bow of Heracles.

Neoptolemus

Will you?

Philoctetes

I shall drive them from it.

Neoptolemus

If you will do what you say,
come now; kiss this ground farewell, and come with me.

(*Heracles appears standing on the rocks above the cave of Philoctetes.*)

Heracles

Not yet, not until you have heard
my words, son of Poias.
I am the voice of Heracles in your ears;   1410
I am the shape of Heracles before you.
It is to serve you I come and leave my home among the dead.
I come
to tell you of the plans of Zeus for you,
to turn you back from the road you go upon.
Hearken to my words.

Let me reveal to you my own story first,
let me show the tasks and sufferings that were mine,
and, at the last, the winning of deathless merit.   1420
All this you can see in me now.
All this must be your suffering too,
the winning of a life to an end in glory,
out of this suffering. Go with this man to Troy.

First, you shall find there the cure of your cruel sickness,
and then be adjudged best warrior among the Greeks.
Paris, the cause of all this evil, you shall kill
with the bow that was mine. Troy you shall take.
You shall win the prize of valor from the army
and shall send the spoils to your home,
to your father Poias, and the land of your fathers, Oeta.   1430
From the spoils of the campaign you must dedicate
some, on my pyre, in memory of my bow.

Son of Achilles, I have the same words for you.
You shall not have the strength to capture Troy
without this man, nor he without you,
but, like twin lions hunting together,
he shall guard you, you him. I shall send Asclepius
to Ilium to heal his sickness. Twice
must Ilium fall to my bow. But this remember,   1440
when you shall come to sack that town, keep holy in the sight of
    God.
All else our father Zeus thinks of less moment.
Holiness does not die with the men that die.
Whether they die or live, it cannot perish.

Philoctetes
Voice that stirs my yearning when I hear,
form lost for so long,
I shall not disobey.

Neoptolemus
Nor I.

Heracles
Do not tarry then.
Season and the tide are hastening you on your way.   1450

Philoctetes
Lemnos, I call upon you:
Farewell, cave that shared my watches,
nymphs of the meadow and the stream,

the deep male growl of the sea-lashed headland
where often, in my niche within the rock,
my head was wet with fine spray,
where many a time in answer to my crying
in the storm of my sorrow the Hermes mountain sent its echo!   1460
Now springs and Lycian well, I am leaving you,
leaving you.
I had never hoped for this.
Farewell Lemnos, sea-encircled,
blame me not but send me on my way
with a fair voyage to where a great destiny
carries me, and the judgment of friends and the all-conquering
Spirit who has brought this to pass.

Chorus

Let us go all
when we have prayed to the nymphs of the sea   1470
to bring us safe to our homes.   1471

THE COMPLETE GREEK TRAGEDIES

AESCHYLUS · I *ORESTEIA*

Translated and with an Introduction by Richmond Lattimore

Agamemnon
The Libation Bearers
The Eumenides

AESCHYLUS · II *FOUR TRAGEDIES*

The Suppliant Maidens. *S. G. Benardete*
The Persians. *S. G. Benardete*
Seven against Thebes. *David Grene*
Prometheus Bound. *David Grene*

SOPHOCLES · I *THREE TRAGEDIES*

Translated and with an Introduction by David Grene

Oedipus the King
Oedipus at Colonus
Antigone

SOPHOCLES · II *FOUR TRAGEDIES*

Ajax. *John Moore*
The Women of Trachis. *Michael Jameson*
Electra *and* Philoctetes. *David Grene*

EURIPIDES · I *FOUR TRAGEDIES*

With an Introduction by Richmond Lattimore

Alcestis. *Richmond Lattimore*
The Medea. *Rex Warner*
The Heracleidae. *Ralph Gladstone*
Hippolytus. *David Grene*

EURIPIDES · II *FOUR TRAGEDIES*

The Cyclops *and* Heracles. *William Arrowsmith*
Iphigenia in Tauris. *Witter Bynner. Introduction by Richmond Lattimore*
Helen. *Richmond Lattimore*

EURIPIDES · III *FOUR TRAGEDIES*

Hecuba. *William Arrowsmith*
Andromache. *John Frederick Nims*
The Trojan Women. *Richmond Lattimore*
Ion. *R. F. Willetts*

EURIPIDES · IV *FOUR TRAGEDIES*

Rhesus. *Richmond Lattimore*
The Suppliant Women. *Frank William Jones*
Orestes. *William Arrowsmith*
Iphigenia in Aulis. *Charles R. Walker*

EURIPIDES · V *THREE TRAGEDIES*

Electra. *Emily Townsend Vermeule*
The Phoenician Women. *Elizabeth Wyckoff*
The Bacchae. *William Arrowsmith*